Locally Grown

LOCALLY GROWN

PORTRAITS OF ARTISANAL FARMS FROM AMERICA'S HEARTLAND

ANNA BLESSING

MIDWAY

AN AGATE IMPRINT

CHICAGO

Printed in China.

All photographs copyright © 2012 Anna Blessing
Design by Brandtner Design.

Library of Congress Cataloging-in-Publication Data

Blessing, Anna H.
  Locally grown : portraits of artisanal farms from America's heartland / Anna H. Blessing.
    p. cm.
  Includes index.
  ISBN-13: 978-1-57284-129-1 (flexibound)
  ISBN-10: 1-57284-129-X (flexibound)
  ISBN-13: 978-1-57284-703-3 (ebook)
  ISBN-10: 1-57284-703-4 (ebook)
1. Agriculture--Middle West. 2. Local foods--Middle West. 3. Farms, Small--Middle West. 4. Farmers--Middle West. 5. Cooking, American. I. Title.
S441.B54 2012
635.0977--dc23
2012008896

10 9 8 7 6 5 4 3 2 1

Midway Books is an imprint of Agate Publishing. Agate books are available in bulk at discount prices. For more information, go to agatepublishing.com.

For Lucia, that you might grow old eating food grown by farmers like these.

ACKNOWLEDGMENTS

The farmers you see in the following pages are my heroes. I am indebted most of all to them, for welcoming me to their farms, and for letting me witness, record, and celebrate their land, their labor, and their art. Thanks also to the busy chefs whose recipes and kind explanations deepened my appreciation of that art. To Doug, who had the confidence to let me explore this project, and to Kate, who brought clarity to every page. To Annie and the friends and family who tested recipes: you helped as much with your enthusiasm as your cooking. And of course to Mom and Shawn, who listened, read, reread, and encouraged me from the start.

TABLE OF CONTENTS

INTRODUCTION

When I set out to do this project, I wanted to show a cross section of artisanal, small-scale farms in the Midwest that are growing food for chefs in Chicago. I talked to a lot of chefs and asked them to name the farmers whom they have worked with often or for a long time, or who were doing creative new things with small-scale agriculture. In other words, standout farmers.

The farmers profiled in these pages are outstanding farmers, but by no means is this list comprehensive; rather, it's a starting point. I hope you'll seek out those exceptional farmers near you and get to know more about them and what they do. You can find them at farmers' markets throughout the city, see their farms' names listed on menus at farm-to-table restaurants, or find them by using the recommended resources in this book.

You'll discover that once you start talking to farmers and chefs about locally grown food, they get pretty excited to tell you about others with whom they have collaborated. One local connection leads to another, and soon you'll find yourself in the middle of the patchwork fabric of the Midwest's local food community, a convergence of people doing similar things in different places that make 200 miles suddenly seem much closer than it did before.

You'll notice that these 20 farms, including three urban farm gardens, vary greatly in size and scale, what they grow or raise, and the methods they use. Small-scale, unique farms like these aren't cookie-cutter in their approach, but the farmers in these pages share a common thread: a desire to grow food in a healthy, thoughtful, intentional way.

All of these farms have forged relationships with chefs in the city of Chicago. This relationship between farmer and chef is about more than a product changing hands from seller to buyer. These are connections formed between two artisans. Nearly every chef will say that meeting farmers in person, talking to them about what they are doing, and visiting their farms are the ways to learn how the food they are buying is grown. A handshake speaks volumes more than a label. An organically certified designation doesn't tell you much about that farmer or his practices, but looking her in the eye, talking to her, meeting her family, seeing her farm—that does.

I encourage you to visit as many farms as you can. It's an incredible thing to see with your own eyes what these farmers are doing—the way these fruits and vegetables are thoughtfully grown and these animals are humanely raised. If you time it right, you may even be able to get your hands dirty helping out on a harvest day.

When I set out to visit farms across the Midwest, I was determined to photograph them as I happened to come upon them, in the moments I happened to be visiting. Some days, the weather was perfect and clear, others it was dreary and muddy (I seemed to time that perfectly to the two days I found myself on pig farms); some days were for pulling vibrantly hued beets from the earth, other days were for weeding or less glorious chores. Regardless of the day or the task, these farmers are there every day working their farms. While I was happy to snap a few harvest shots (check out the garlic at Leaning Shed Farm, and the carrots at Genesis Growers!), other shots show the farms at a moment in time, sometimes before fruit has matured on the tree, or sometimes when tomatoes have been ripening past their peak on the vines.

These farms are about working with nature on a human scale, and using all of her coolest tricks and amazing systems to grow food. That means that rows are not pristine and perfectly weed-free, fruits and vegetables are not one size and shape, animals run around outdoors, and everything along the path, from the soil to the city, is affected by the weather. Farming is the taming of nature to a certain extent, but the beauty in these farms comes from that fine line of some, and zero, control. **— Anna Blessing**

HOW TO USE THIS BOOK

Each chapter is dedicated to a farm. The chapters are organized into four sections, grouping together like farms—the family farms, the new farms started by urban transplants, the farms that aren't defined by either, and urban farms in Chicago. Each chapter can stand alone; you can read this book from beginning to end, or you can jump around and read the chapters out of order. At the end of each chapter, you will find two sections: From the Farmer and From the Chef.

FROM THE FARMER

In addition to the story that I tell through my words and photographs from visiting each farm, I've also asked the farmers to contribute to their chapters. Many of them have contributed a favorite recipe or food preparation, and many have included their personal resources—books, blogs, films, or organizations that have inspired, helped, or supported them along the way.

FROM THE CHEF

Chefs throughout the city, at big hotel restaurants and small indie spots alike, work with these farmers weekly through much of the year. I asked the farmers to name the chefs they worked with frequently, and I asked those chefs to contribute recipes, so you can see what Bruce Sherman, Carlos Ysaguirre, Sarah Stegner, and others like to do with these incredible products.

CONTRIBUTING CHEFS

Buying Locally, Cooking Locally

It's hard to find a chef of note in Chicago who *doesn't* source locally, but many of them are especially dedicated to supporting the local food system and farmers, who are equally dedicated to them. The following chefs who have contributed recipes throughout the book have shared their thoughts on locally grown food.

DUNCAN BIDDULPH, ROOTSTOCK

You start to do something because it's the way you're taught or because you feel it's the right thing, and as you learn more about the farmers and you learn more about how they are doing it, then you get a sense about why it's so important. There are more reasons than I could name as to why I do it, like supporting small little operations and how that kind of spreads out and supports economies of all sizes. When you can get anything from anywhere by just placing a phone call or clicking on a website, it makes it more special to get something that you can put a face to; you understand that a lot of people are putting a good deal of effort into what they're doing.

PAUL FEHRIBACH, BIG JONES

I think that healthy eating is eating food that is fresh. We can certainly scientifically figure out an antibiotic or chemical that will have this or that impact, we can develop drugs or technology, but when it comes to food there is nothing we can do to put away millions of years of evolution. We are genetically programmed to eat straight from the earth. And I don't think that there is any way to substitute that. There is nothing that science can do to replace a natural diet that comes from the area surrounding you.

CLEETUS FRIEDMAN, CITY PROVISIONS

When I came up with a business model, it was a question of what can I do that's gonna make me pour out my passion, pour out my personality, but also have a really big sense of community. That's the base of my business model: Create a very short lane between where food comes from and where it is consumed, and enable a connection. Because I really see food and people and community automatically happening, but if you can push just a little further and connect people—I can walk around this store and tell you about every single person and where he comes from and why she's here. It took a lot of work, but this is a culmination of the relationships. I'm lucky that people understand this local food movement. Without getting too political or religious, my approach to life is the belief that God is in everything, and I think that relates to my culinary philosophy, which is respecting that which you cook with. Collectively, we are here to pay homage to the gift of life and the gift of food.

JASON HAMMEL, NIGHTWOOD AND LULA CAFE

What got me started was the excitement of it. I got going in the early days of the farm-to-table movement, so it was almost a more radical thing to do. The farmers' markets were poorly attended and cold and rainy and not the scene that they are today; it felt like I was exploring a new place, and once I got there it was clearly the best place to be. We are always searching for the best products we can find, and when I realized I could get my hands on locally sourced stuff, that became the passion. Today, it's still the best—not always 99 percent of the time, but mostly—and I have developed really important relationships, friendships, and partnerships with these farmers, and that is one of the reasons to be in a business like this.

BRIAN HUSTON, THE PUBLICAN

I spent some time in San Francisco cooking at Zuni Café, and that exposed me to the whole market and working with farmers directly. I discovered this whole hidden aspect of cooking that I didn't know existed: making friends. Having a good relationship with the mushroom guy with the dirty hands at the back door, or the farmer who grew the romaine for the Caesar salad who I could ask to grow it a little bigger or smaller, as opposed to that one big truck making a drop off. It's a nice break in the day when we work so long and hard to have those little moments.

STEPHANIE IZARD, GIRL AND THE GOAT

It's all about supporting local, but when you can actually go to the farmers' markets and meet the family and see the story you get more excited about it. Before opening Girl and the Goat, we went to most every farm that we use, picked vegetables and milked cows and made cheese. I think it gives you a better appreciation for the work that goes into every beet or every little thing you use that someone handpicked—and it's kind of a pain in the ass! It's not like mass-produced foods that are picked by some kind of machinery. I didn't realize how hard it is until I tried to do it myself.

PAUL KAHAN, AVEC, BLACKBIRD, THE PUBLICAN, AND BIG STAR

For me, it's all I know, it's the only way I know how to cook. We are inspired first and foremost by the ingredients, and the best way to find those ingredients is to go to your farmers' market or to work with great farmers. The food they are growing dictates the direction the food in our restaurants goes. It's a really huge priority for us to know where our food comes from, and that is paramount, but for me also what makes food and wine and my profession so interesting are the stories that go along with the people who grow and raise this food. I find that farmers are really intelligent. They explore their passions, and the only way to be a successful farmer is to be smart and to find a niche and do things that no one else is doing.

CHRIS PANDEL, THE BRISTOL AND BALENA

For me it's about the relationships. We are in the business of making people happy, entertaining them and feeding them, and in order for me to be happy doing that, I need to know the people we are doing business with, from customers to farmers. The farmers are the most important people in terms of the food, and the relationships we have are fairly intimate, so we can create dishes based on food specific to our restaurant—some farmers grow things especially for us, and that gives us a chance to be different solely based on the product we have. From there we try not to adulterate anything, so that everything we do is to accent whatever the farmers did.

SEAN SANDERS, BROWNTROUT

I want to bring in good quality ingredients, I want to support local farmers, I want to create an economy within our own means. Rather than outsourcing meat and vegetables and relying on a meat supplier, I rely on a farmer. F me it's about creating our own local economy. It makes a lot of sense to me to do something local and support your own economy and do things that will be a blessing for everyone in your economy.

PATRICK SHEERIN, TRENCHERMEN

I consider myself very fortunate to cook in Chicago because my colleagues are amazing, because you can ask them for anything, and you can say who do you get this from and they'll tell you that farm and another three. In our hearts, chefs want the system to change. If we're involved in this, we want everyone to eat better, and we want it to be shared with everyone. It's just a great time to cook in Chicago because we have great access to these local foods and people are not competitive about it.

BRUCE SHERMAN, NORTH POND

Ultimately for me, it's about flavor and taste, and as a professional cook, I was looking for the product because it tasted better. The stuff that was grown responsibly and carefully and with love tasted better. It's the notion that local food tastes better because it's local and it's not traveling across the country to get here. As a cook, as a father, as an adult, as a citizen, my concern for seeking local product was broader, for my kids, for my grandkids, for the society at large. I wanted to feel like I was doing the right thing. Deep down. It's feeling good about what we use and where it's coming from, and the fact that other people are concerned about it or sourcing it. And that's going to raise all the boats in the harbor, when we get people who are coming to the market who are concerned about what they're eating for the reasons of health, for health of their bodies, health of the earth.

SARAH STEGNER, PRAIRIE GRASS CAFE

To start with it's always come down to taste for me. I want to do the best job that I can in what I serve to customers, and over and over again the products that are handled correctly from beginning to end, are very fresh, and that come from a local source are the ones that taste best. That's been the driving force, but there is also a sense of doing the right thing by protecting our land and ensuring there will be land to farm for future generations in our area.

JARED VAN CAMP, OLD TOWN SOCIAL AND NELLCÔTE

When I started cooking, the reason to go to farmers' markets wherever I was working at that time was very simple: it was because the produce was better. It wasn't this trend, or "I'm gonna go to the market because it's cool"—it was a necessity because the produce was simply better. You could find better tomatoes from a farmer than you could from a produce company.

PAUL VIRANT, PERENNIAL VIRANT AND VIE

Sourcing locally was one of the major missions of Vie when we started. I had some connections with a few farmers. I had worked with Paul Kahan at Blackbird, and there was a whole set of farmers he worked with. That particular culture was new to me at the time, and it really helped seal the deal with what we would do at Vie, and now over the course of the year, we work with 40 farmers.

CARLOS YSAGUIRRE, ACRE AND ANTEPRIMA

I've always felt it was our obligation, as chefs, to source out the best ingredients possible. And if it's grown right in the backyard, it probably tastes a lot better. When people ask me why, it's more like why wouldn't I want to source locally? It's better for us, better for the restaurant, better for people. I've built relationships with these farmers, and it's a wonderful community to be a part of.

ANDREW ZIMMERMAN, SEPIA

I try to buy from farmers because it just tastes better. That is the starting point. The fact that it's local and sustainable or organic, those are all great bonuses, but the fact of the matter is that it tastes great. Once you move past that into other reasons, it all just falls into place.

RANDY ZWEIBAN, PROVINCE

I always wanted to do farm-to-table cuisine. I grew up with a deep appreciation for having a garden where we had our own tomatoes and basil. I always had an appreciation for making good food and eating good food. Here in August, who doesn't want to eat a tomato or ear of corn that comes from here? It's perfect. The growing weather is perfect; it's the time of year for that harvest. The challenge is sourcing what you can locally and embracing that, but realizing you're still a restaurant in downtown Chicago.

PART 1

REFASHIONING THE FAMILY FARM

M any of the family farms that once made up an elaborate patchwork of land across the Midwest have struggled to compete in the world of industrial farming, and when their neighbors got big, they got out. ✳ Luckily, several family farms did survive, and older farmers have passed along their knowledge to the next generations. In the following seven chapters, the current generation that has inherited these farms has found a way to make them viable in today's environment by growing specialty crops, working closely with chefs, caring for market customers, raising animals humanely, using organic practices, and returning to traditional methods of farming the land. Whether these farmers are recuperating the health of the soil that was at one time farmed conventionally, like Spence Farm, or continuing an organic approach to growing, like Henry's Farm, they are impressive in their progress toward creating healthy food and healthy land by using traditional, artisanal methods.

INPUTSUNA
MONGOLIAN
HENRY'S FAVORITE
Chives $2
STIR-FRY VEGETABLE
Red Beets $3

CHAPTER 1

BECKER LANE ORGANIC FARM

Jude Becker | Dyersville, Iowa | beckerlaneorganic.com

Just outside the little town of Dyersville, Iowa, sits the site for the filming of the motion picture *Field of Dreams*. A sign staked along Route 136 will point you east to the location, where you can bat a ball and run the bases. But if you drive a few miles north, at the very end of Becker Lane, you'll find a different sort of site amid the cornfields, where Jude Becker has built his own field of dreams.

Jude is a sixth-generation hog farmer, running a family farm that dates back to 1850. Influenced by the history of his family and inspired by a system from England that allows him to sustainably raise 5,000 pigs a year, he has built it, and it seems that from all accounts, they are coming.

Though Jude has singlehandedly revitalized the farm into an organic, year-round pig farm rooted in biodynamic philosophies, the generations before him maintained the traditional integrity of the farm, and despite the changing landscape around them, the family never made the change to industrial methods. By the 1980s, the farm was struggling to keep its head above water in a sea of industrialized farms.

In college at Iowa State in the late '90s, Jude began to formulate a plan to save the family farm. "My family has always celebrated food," he says. "And I felt like I ought to as well."

He started small with six sows, or female pigs, in the summer of 1999. Just a few summers later he started selling to Whole Foods Market, which was looking for domestic, organic pork. Jude grew the business from six sows to 100. In 2007, he grew the farm even bigger when Whole Foods increased its demand and he began selling to La Quercia, an artisanal cured meats company in Iowa, as well as a handful of restaurants in Chicago. Jude grew his pig population to 350 sows. By breeding those sows in a regular rotation, he found he could produce 100 pigs a week.

Although Jude had, in a matter of eight years, dramatically increased the farm's size and production, it wasn't until 2008 when Becker Lane Organic Farm gained national traction in the kitchens of some of the best restaurants in the country. "Oprah decided to do a story about animal welfare, and she called us," Jude says. "After we were on that show, I became very well known in California, and it was really easy for us to put together a big collection of restaurants there. That allowed us to get a lot more scope and diverse market base which gave me some independence."

After that, Becker Lane organic pork started showing up at eateries and upscale groceries in Northern California. Alice Waters put Becker Lane on her menu at Chez Panisse. Zuni Café in San Francisco followed. Soon Becker Lane hogs were going to 25 restaurants in the Bay Area and more than a dozen in Chicago, where Paul Kahan was ordering a pig a week from Jude for his new pork-centric gastropub, The Publican.

THE PROCESS

Jude will tell you that he farms on the right side of his brain, but don't let that fool you. He may approach the process as an art form, but his farm is one of the most rational, organized systems you can imagine. The fact that Jude farms 340 acres organically, with a team of four, to produce 5,000 humanely raised pigs a year is testament to the left-brained logic that reigns Becker Lane.

"I took a lot of my ideas of doing things from my family, but working in Europe for a few months really helped me out," Jude says.

"Europe is about 20 years ahead of us on this whole sustainable animal evolution," he explains. "They've worked out some systems for managing the farm, especially the work schedule. What I learned allows us to be as big and stable as we are. When Paul Kahan needs pork, he needs it every week. And a lot of farmers haven't figured that out yet."

The cycle on Jude's farm starts with the sows who are artificially insemi-nated and give birth year-round, so that each week he has pigs to sell. A

The male piglets are weaned at seven weeks and moved to open-air hoop barns where they are fattened on organic corn and soybeans.

computer program records the data and spits out projections, including the expected birthing day for impregnated sows. A week before a sow is expected to farrow, or give birth to her piglets, an alert is emailed to Jude and his crew to move the sows to an individual farrowing hut (he has 55) and patch of land. When it's time, the sows are moved, new piglets are born, and seven weeks later, they are weaned.

The male piglets are castrated and moved to open hoop barns or smaller, portable open-air structures where they are fattened with a diet of organic corn and soybeans for the next 7 months. The gilts, or young females who haven't yet given birth, go back into the breeding cycle, and the whole process begins anew. All the pigs are raised in a way where they can express their nature—rolling in mud when it's hot, building nests out of straw when they're farrowing, rooting around in the grass, and spending their days out of doors.

RESULTS

There is a lot of thought, philosophy, and organization that goes into Becker Lane, but in the end, Jude produces unbelievably tasty pork. He is often asked why it tastes so good.

"For me, there are three factors," Jude says. "First, these animals live in a free environment, not in their own stink. That smell engrains itself into the meat and that ruins flavor. I can't quantify that, but in this free space, there is no bad smell. Second, the food they eat is organic. Pigs convert anything into meat, whatever you put back in you get back out. Finally, it's the genetics. The Cheshire-Berkshire genetics are a great genetic background for meat quality."

Jude looks out to the pasture at his pigs. "People come here and think there is something magical here; there's no magic. It's just people who want to take care of animals, have an organized, thought-out plan to do it, and follow through on the plan."

GET A TASTE OF BECKER LANE ORGANIC FARM

NORTH POND
northpondrestaurant.com

PROVINCE
provincerestaurant.com

THE PUBLICAN
thepublicanrestaurant.com

THE PURPLE PIG
thepurplepigchicago.com

SPIAGGIA
spiaggiarestaurant.com

TERZO PIANO
terzopianochicago.com

TRENCHERMEN

Jude says straw is a crucial element for the pigs, who spend time playing with, manipulating, and making beds out of it.

FROM THE FARMER: Jude Becker

RESOURCES AND INSPIRATION

Cato, Varro, and Columella were ancient Roman writers who wrote on Roman agriculture; they had a clear-headed approach and provided a framework for me to build my philosophy on. The Roman way of organized farming on a serious scale without modern industrialization invokes great sentiment within me.

Alice Waters's books are so inspirational, and have a way of being a light to guide me when other lights have gone out.

Highgrove: An Experiment in Organic Gardening and Farming **by HRH Prince of Wales and Charles Clover** inspired me to enter organic farming when I read it in the '90s. The idea was to be serious about food and direct marketing, not just the farm process or being cheap.

BECKER LANE PORK BELLY
WITH CARAMELIZED ONION RICE CAKES AND PICKLED CABBAGE SALAD
By **Patrick Sheerin,** Trenchermen
4–6 SERVINGS

"This is one of those great fall dishes: pork belly, caramelized onions, and the amazing cabbages really in season. It's the flavors and foods I crave in late October. We really like using Savoy cabbage because of the beautiful texture and flavor. Becker Lane organic pork is really well marbled—the bellies especially are nicely streaked with fat and meat, and they taste like pork."—Patrick Sheerin

Note: Making pork belly is a two-day process and will yield extra meat.

Pork Belly
3 ounces (85 g) kosher salt
1 ounce (28 g) toasted black peppercorns, roughly crushed
1 ounce (28 g) brown sugar
1 (2-pound [908-g]) piece Becker Lane pork belly (skin off)
1 cup (237 mL) chicken stock
2 sprigs of thyme

Rice Cakes
6 tablespoons (90 mL) canola oil
2 large Spanish onions
Salt
3 cloves garlic, thinly sliced
2 cups (380 g) uncooked Arborio rice
½ cup (119 mL) white wine
8 cups (1.90 L) vegetable stock
¼ cup (25 g) thinly sliced green onions
½ pound (227 g) scamorza cheese, shredded
1 cup (250 g) rice flour
Pickled Cabbage Salad (recipe follows)
Hazelnut Vinaigrette (recipes follows)
Chopped toasted hazelnuts, for garnish

(Continued on next page)

1. Begin pork belly preparation the day before serving. Mix the salt, crushed peppercorns, and brown sugar. Rub the pork belly with the mixture, wrap in plastic wrap, and place in a pie plate in the refrigerator overnight.

2. Begin the rice cakes preparation the day before serving. Heat 3 tablespoons (45 mL) of the oil in a non-reactive Dutch oven over medium heat. Add the onions and a pinch of salt and cook on low heat, stirring every 2 to 3 minutes. It will take nearly 1½ hours to develop a deep rich caramelization of the onions. Add a tablespoon of water every once in a while if it starts to get dark on the bottom of the pan.

3. When the onions are a deep golden brown color, increase the heat to medium, add the garlic, and sweat for 1 minute. Stir in the rice. When the rice starts "sticking" to the pan, add the white wine and cook until it is absorbed by the rice. Simmer the vegetable stock and add, 2 cups (474 mL) at a time, stirring with a wooden spoon until the stock is absorbed before adding more. Cook until the rice kernels are just about cooked through. This process will take approximately 15 to 25 minutes.

4. Once the rice is just about cooked, season to taste with salt. Remove from the heat and let stand 5 minutes. Fold in the green onions, then the cheese with just a few stirs to keep the cheese intact as much as possible. Place the rice mixture in a loaf pan lined with plastic wrap, smooth the top, fold the plastic wrap over the rice, and place another loaf pan filled with ice on top. Refrigerate overnight.

5. Early on the day of serving, rinse the pork belly, place in a covered ovenproof Dutch oven with the chicken stock and thyme, and bake in a 225°F (110°C) oven until just tender, 3 to 4 hours,. Let cool to room temperature in the broth.

6. While the pork belly is cooling, prepare the Hazelnut Vinaigrette and the Pickled Cabbage Salad.

7. Drain the pork belly and pat dry with paper towels. Cut the belly in half. (Save one half for another use.) Wipe out the pan and heat over medium-low heat. Score the fat of the remaining pork belly and sear the belly in the Dutch oven until golden brown, then turn over. Bake at 250°F (120°C) 20 minutes or until heated through. Let rest 5 minutes, then cut into ¼-inch [6-mm] slices, 2 per person.

8. While the pork belly is baking, remove the rice mixture from the loaf pan and cut the loaf into 4 (1-inch [2.5-cm]) slices. (Save the remaining loaf for another day.) Cut the slices in half to form rectangles, dust with rice flour, and sear in batches in the remaining 3 tablespoons (45 mL) oil in a nonstick skillet until golden brown and delicious. Place in a 200°F (90°C) oven to keep warm.

9. To plate, divide the Pickled Cabbage Salad among 4 pasta bowls. Place the rice cakes to the side and the pork belly on top. Drizzle with additional vinaigrette and garnish with hazelnuts.

HAZELNUT VINAIGRETTE

½ cup (119 mL) chardonnay vinegar
¼ cup (59 mL) Dijon mustard
¾ cup (178 mL) canola oil
¾ cup (178 mL) hazelnut oil
Salt and pepper, to taste

1. Whisk together the vinegar and mustard, then whisk the oils until the mixture is emulsified. Season to taste with salt and black pepper.

PICKLED CABBAGE SALAD

1 cup (142 g) fresh sauerkraut
1 cup (90 g) chiffonade savoy cabbage
1 tablespoon freshly minced chives
Hazelnut Vinaigrette
Salt and pepper

1. Rinse the sauerkraut and place on paper towels. Press to remove excess liquid. Place sauerkraut, cabbage, and chives in a bowl. Add enough vinaigrette to moisten the ingredients, reserving some for serving, and toss the salad. Season to taste with salt and pepper.

MORTEAU SAUSAGE

By **Paul Kahan and Brian Huston**, The Publican

"Jude Becker is a visionary, and first and foremost his pork is the best tasting pork I've ever had. His farm is an amazing place, and the animals we get from him are unparalleled in quality and flavor, and he will tell you it's different because of the way they are raised."—Paul Kahan

> 1 (10-pound [4.54-kg]) pork shoulder
> ¼ cup (75 g) salt
> 10 juniper berries
> 6 allspice berries
> 1 tablespoon cayenne pepper
> 1 tablespoon dried thyme
> 1 tablespoon granulated garlic
> 1 tablespoon Espelette pepper or hot paprika
> ½ tablespoon cure (#1 cure or nitrate curing salt) (optional)
> ½ tablespoon dry mustard powder
> ½ tablespoon granulated onion
> 1 teaspoon ground mace
> 1 teaspoon ground cloves

1. Cut pork into 1-inch (2.5-cm) cubes and mix with all the other ingredients. Let meat marinate overnight in the refrigerator.

2. Before grinding, place meat in freezer 30 minutes, or until almost frozen.

3. Grind meat on a medium die. Using a mixer with a paddle attachment, emulsify the ground meat by paddling it for 2 minutes or until meat is sticky and paler in color. Stuff the meat into hog casings or in place of bulk sausage. Store in the refrigerator for up to 7 days.

CHAPTER 2

GREEN ACRES FARM

Beth and Brent Eccles | North Judson, Indiana | greenacresindiana.com

Most weeks from spring to fall, the Green Acres market stall at Green City Market is one of the largest, crates and baskets overflowing with nearly 500 different varieties of heirloom vegetables. Eggplants, peppers, turnips, tomatoes, potatoes, melons, Asian and Italian specialty cooking greens, asparagus, peas, sorrel, stinging nettle, lamb's quarters, kales, chards, choys, spinaches, turnips, beets, radishes, hard winter squashes—the bounty spilling out onto the market tables week after week during peak harvest is incredible.

As one of the bigger, more prolific farms to supply market customers and Chicago chefs, it's hard to imagine that at one time Beth and Brent once showed up at a farmers' market, unfamiliar and unsure of what to do, without even a tent or a table.

THE FAMILY FARM

Beth's grandparents were immigrants from Japan in the late 1800s. Their arranged marriage was in California, where they started a little farm growing strawberries. After a drought wiped them out, along with many other farms, they migrated east toward Chicago, and started working on a farm not far from North Judson, where Green Acres Farm sits today.

Eventually Beth's grandparents bought their own 200-acre farm, just down the road from where Green Acres sits today, and began growing Asian vegetables, things like Japanese radishes and Chinese bitter melon. Beth's grandfather would drive his pickup truck to Chicago's Chinatown and deliver out of his truck.

Beth's father took over the family business and expanded Beth's grandparents' original farm, still focusing on specialty Asian vegetables. He grew Korean radishes that he sold to the big places in the city processing kimchi, his harvest coming off on big pallets at the South Water Market.

"Even though it was a small family farm," Beth says, "there wasn't that connection to people. We had a few big customers who were buying everything." Beth says it worked well for her dad, but when she and Brent took over the farm, they realized they needed—and wanted—to do something different.

THE BEGINNINGS

Beth and Brent were living in Indianapolis, where they had a garden. Beth was working for a group of professors and on her lunch breaks she would head to the Indianapolis city market and peddle plants she was growing in her dad's greenhouses on his farm. "I never pictured myself coming back to the farm and really farming," Beth says, "but I could never picture myself sitting inside an office, either."

Soon after Beth and Brent had their first daughter, Beth's parents suggested they buy a farm that had come up for sale close to theirs. "We just kind of bought the farm and came up here. It was the craziest thing, and if you believe in destiny or God or that things work out, there was definitely some of that there."

They started farming in 1996 with Beth's dad—working on his land and theirs—and discovered it was getting harder and harder to survive. "My dad had a wholesale business that put my brother and me through college," Beth says, "but when he retired he was still selling a box of radishes for the same price that he was when he started 40 years ago. The cost of everything else had gone up—labor, boxes—so he wasn't really making any money."

Beth's dad had been invited to an annual market called the Best of the Midwest for several years and had never gone. "He handed us the card and said maybe you should contact this lady and go," Beth says. "And it was Abby Mandel, who started Green City Market." Beth and Brent were the only ones there with unusual Asian vegetable varieties. "We had a lot of interest, a lot of people handing us cards," Beth says.

Brent prepares a field for planting; Black Futsu squash and basil are late summer harvest at Green Acres.

BLACK FUTSU

One woman was particularly persistent. Neither Beth nor Brent knew anything about farmers' markets, but the woman running the Downers Grove market encouraged them to finish the season at her market.

"We had no idea what was involved," Beth says, laughing. "I don't think we even had tables or tents. We had all of our stuff in baskets sitting on the ground, because that is the way we harvested it. But we sold everything we had."

They finished out the year at the market and did well. The following year they sold at the Federal and Daley Plaza markets, the two biggest city markets at the time.

CHANGING THE FARM

Green Acres is 155 acres, with 35 acres of woods. Beth says each season they till and plant about 40 acres and leave the rest in cover crops as part of a crop rotation to let the land rest.

"My dad was farming every available piece." Beth says, "He would plant a whole section in radishes, where we might do just two rows of something."

Beth's dad had farmed conventionally, occasionally using synthetic fertilizers. "But we didn't want to do that," Beth says. "We had been into the organic movement and wanted to grow organically."

Growing organically means more hands needed in the field to weed. Green Acres Farm employs nine workers through the H-2A temporary agriculture program, which secures legal workers from different countries to work on the farm.

Though Brent had no farming in his background, he enjoyed working out of doors, and with an engineering background, he could fix any broken piece of equipment. He learned to plant and plow from Beth's dad, then Beth and Brent started to grow a sustainable farm by using natural fertilizers like fish, seaweed, and molasses, and by planting nutrient-rich cover crops such as green manure.

Beth says they also knew they didn't want a wholesale farm. After they experienced the markets, seeing both the excitement from people as well as the money they could make, the choice was clear.

CHEFS AT MARKET

Patrick Sheerin first started buying from Green Acres when they were still at the Federal Plaza Farmers' Market. The first time he approached Beth, she said no. "It was the first time I was told that I couldn't have something at the market," says Patrick, who was buying vegetables in large quantities for the Signature Room at the 95th, where he was chef at the time.

"Green Acres had this golden zucchini that I had never seen before. The squash that they grow, the variety and flavors, are just unreal, and I really wanted the golden. I asked, 'Can I have 20 pounds of this?' and Beth said, 'No, I need it all for Bruce Sherman.'" Patrick smiles. "I was like, wow, alright. She wasn't trying to be rude, but she said, 'How often are you going to buy from me? We need to be in a relationship.' So I said ok, let's work on that relation-

ship." Now Patrick is one of their most consistent customers.

After 9/11, the Federal Plaza Farmers' Market was shut down, and Abby Mandel asked Brent and Beth to come to her Wednesday market in Lincoln Park.

"Abby's whole vision was the chef-farmer connection," Beth says. "And who knew that it would become what it is today. Ninety-nine percent of our connections have come from Green City Market—that's amazing."

Every week they send an email out to more than 150 chefs describing what will be at the market that week. Tony Priolo at Piccolo Sogno, Greg Biggers at The Sofitel Hotel, and Patrick Sheerin, are some of Green Acres's biggest customers. Beth says nearly every chef who orders from them picks up at the market. "They're not just shopping with us, they're supporting other farms," Beth says. "And there are vegetables they won't know about unless they walk through our booth, like burgundy okra; it's this little hot item that's never going to be on that email list. Chefs have to show up early to get that." Beth says all of the chefs like those extremely niche treasures they grow.

Any given market day, you're likely to see chefs like Jason Hammel from Nightwood and Lula Cafe, Bill Kim from Urban Belly and Belly Shack, and Carlos Ysaguirre of Acre and Anteprima, perusing the vast array of varieties at Green Acres and adding to their orders with those small specialty vegetables they would never know about without showing up in person.

FROM THE FARMERS: Beth and Brent Eccles

RESOURCES AND INSPIRATION

We certified our farm with a fantastic organization, **Certified Naturally Grown** (naturallygrown.org). They represent a grass-roots alternative to being certified organic. The certification is farmer-based rather than government-regulated. They do not charge you based on gross income, but rather what you feel you can afford to donate yearly.

In 2004, our farm was chosen, along with two others, to represent **Slow Food Chicago** (slowfoodchicago.org) at the Slow Food World Conference in Turin, Italy. It was a great experience!

Mott Family Farm (mottfamilyfarm.com). My cousin, Shelley Sakaguchi Mott, along with her husband, Jeff, and their three sons began farming in Salesville, Ohio, in 2005. Basically the family of five along with a few part-time Amish helpers and an occasional intern, make this small, family farm very unique. Shelley was a theater major at UCLA, a true city girl. The life changes she has made are fascinating, and she writes a great blog.

We attend the **ACRES USA** (acresusa.com) yearly farm conference. It is a great organization that supports and encourages sustainable farming.

WATERMELON SALAD

By **Chris Pandel**, The Bristol and Balena

4–6 SERVINGS

3 ounces (85 g) cubed watermelon

Salt and pepper, to taste

2 ounces (57 g) Marinated Feta (recipe follows)

1 tablespoon pickled shallot or onion

10 parsley leaves

5 mint leaves

3 basil leaves

2 ounces (57 g) Black Olive Vinaigrette (recipe follows)

1. Place the watermelon seasoned to taste with salt and pepper on serving plates. Place the Marinated Feta on top. Cover with pickled shallot, herbs, and black olive vinaigrette. Serve chilled.

MARINATED FETA

½ pound (227 g) block feta cheese

6 leaves basil, chopped

1 tablespoon chopped parsley

Pinch pepper

2 tablespoons olive oil

1. Blend herbs, pepper, and oil together with a couple cubes of ice. Cover cheese for 24 hours.

BLACK OLIVE VINAIGRETTE

1½ cups (356 mL) grape seed oil

1 cup (237 mL) olive oil

1 cup (237 mL) red wine vinegar

1 cup (134 g) crushed black olives, pitted

3 tablespoons (24 g) fried capers

2 shallots, minced

1 tablespoon sugar

1 teaspoon garam masala

1. Combine all ingredients.

CRISPY CAVOLO NERO KALE AND PECORINO ROMANO

By **Carlos Ysaguirre**, Acre and Anteprima

4–6 SERVINGS

"Brent and Beth have always been great supporters. People usually say the chefs are the ones that support the farmers, but I see things a bit differently. Their passion and dedication shine in their produce and we are more than grateful that they allow us to bring that into the restaurant."—Carlos Ysaguirre

2 pounds (908 g) cavolo nero kale, rinsed and thoroughly dried
2 cups (474 mL) olive oil
½ pound (227 g) piece Pecorino Romano, grated
Zest of 2 lemons
Fine sea salt, to taste

EQUIPMENT
1 deep sauté pan
1 microplane or fine zester
1 candy thermometer
1 webbed strainer for drawing out cavolo from hot oil

1. Cut kale into 2-inch (5-cm) pieces.

2. Pour the olive oil into a large saucepan and heat to 350°F (180°C). Working in batches, add enough of the kale to fit comfortably in the hot oil without overcrowding. Fry until crisp, about 2 minutes, or until the oil stops bubbling. (Do not overcook or the kale will burn.) With a webbed strainer remove the kale from oil and drain on paper towels. Working quickly, transfer the hot kale to a large bowl and toss with some of the Pecorino Romano and lemon zest, and season to taste with the sea salt. Repeat the process with the rest of the kale. Serve while still warm.

WINTER SQUASH SOUP

WITH GRILLED FRISÉE, TAMARIND, CHILI OIL, COCOA NIBS, AND ROSEMARY

By **Jason Hammel**, Nightwood and Lula Cafe

12 SERVINGS

"We like to use violina rugulosa winter squash from Green Acres Farm. Any of the fun Italian butternut squash heirloom varieties will work too."—Jason Hammel

Chili Oil (recipe follows)
6 butternut squash, peeled, cut into chunks
12 red onions, unpeeled, halved
½ cup (119 mL) sherry vinegar
¼ cup (59 mL) extra-virgin olive oil
4 tablespoons (59 mL) tamarind syrup, plus small amount for drizzle
3 tablespoons (45 mL) maple syrup
½ teaspoon tamarind concentrate
2½ teaspoons salt
½ pound (227 g) unsalted butter
4 bulbs fennel, diced
1 cup (165 g) golden raisins
1-inch (2.5-cm) piece gingerroot, minced
1 tablespoon ground cumin
½ teaspoon ground coriander
½ teaspoon ground cardamom
½ teaspoon ground mace
½ teaspoon ground juniper berries
8 quarts (7.58 L) chicken or vegetable stock
½ bottle Riesling wine
Champagne vinegar
Grilled Frisée, for garnish (recipe follows)
Chopped rosemary leaves, for garnish
Cocoa nibs, for garnish
Additional tamarind syrup

1. Prepare Chili Oil.

2. Place squash and onions on a rimmed baking sheet. Whisk together the vinegar, oil, tamarind syrup, maple syrup, and tamarind concentrate in a bowl and drizzle over the vegetables. Season with the salt. Roast at 350°F (180°C) until vegetables are tender and caramelized.

3. Melt the butter in a large soup pot over low heat. Add the fennel, raisins, ginger, and spices and stir briefly. Cover and sweat until fennel is translucent. Deglaze with Riesling. Add roasted vegetables and the stock. Heat to boiling, reduce heat, and simmer 1 hour.

4. Season to taste with additional salt and champagne vinegar.

5. Prepare Grilled Frisée.

6. To serve, ladle soup into bowls. Top with rosemary, cocoa nibs, and a few small pieces of the torn frisée. Finish with a drizzle of tamarind syrup and Chili Oil.

CHILI OIL

    4 ancho chilies
    ½ cup (119 mL) olive oil

1. Rehydrate the chilies. Puree with as little water as possible in a blender to form a paste. Spread on a nonstick baking pan. Bake at 250°F (120°C) 2 hours, or until the paste is dark and nearly burnt. Cool. Transfer to a spice grinder and process into a fine powder and whisk into oil.

GRILLED FRISÉE

    1 head frisée
    ¼ cup (59 mL) oil

1. Prepare grill. Drizzle oil over frisée and grill for 15 to 20 seconds.

★

CHAPTER **3**

GUNTHORP FARMS

Greg Gunthorp | LaGrange, Indiana | gunthorpfarms.com

You can tell it isn't the first time Greg Gunthorp has told the story of his fourth-generation farm and how he came to have a USDA-approved processing plant on it—an enormous feat for any small farm.

"My family has raised pigs for four generations. I grew up on the next road over. My grandpa and grandma moved down in the mid-'50s when the toll road came through. My family has always raised pigs the same way, with the sows with their babies farrowing outside in the fields and the pigs outside their whole lives. We've always raised a few chickens. We got into chickens big for Rick Bayless and Frontera. And the first customer we sold to was Charlie Trotter."

He pauses, and gives a big, impish grin.

"Pretty good place to start, right?"

Though Gunthorp Farms, in LaGrange, Indiana, had raised pigs for generations, it wasn't until 1998 that the farm started selling to restaurants in Chicago.

"In 1998 I sold my pigs for less than what my grandpa sold them for during the Depression," Greg says. Everyone around him said he couldn't survive, continuing to farm the way he always had.

"I guess I'm kind of stubborn. When I get my mind set on something and someone tells me I'm not going to do it, I'm going to do it," Greg says, grinning again.

A CHANGING LANDSCAPE

Greg is strong-willed and determined, with a lot of ideas about agriculture. He likes to do things his way, and isn't one to back down when he's told no. But his manner is soft; the mischievous glint he gets in his eye is part rebel teen, part jolly old St. Nick. And his end goal is always that of producing food in a humane, conscientious way. The bigger the challenge before him, the more apt Greg seems to be to take it on.

After speaking on sustainable agriculture at a conference in Missouri, Greg met a few guys afterward. One of them had a friend in Oregon who was raising pigs and shipping them to Chicago. "He said his friend was going to quit and that the restaurant was looking for a pig farmer," Greg remembers. "So I called, and it was Charlie Trotter's."

Suddenly Greg had a clientele for his pastured pigs, which could fetch two to three times as much as commodity pigs.

The Gunthorps may never have changed their farming methods, but the world around them did, forcing Greg to carve out a way to survive farming, on a manageable scale. Pig farmers around him were quitting or transforming their farms into major operations where pigs were raised indoors in crowded barns. "When I was a teenager, in the early '80s, there were 600,000 pigs farmers in the United States," Greg says. "That dropped to under 60,000 last year. In my lifetime, 90 percent of the pig farms have disappeared." The number of total pigs produced, however, has not decreased.

THE PIGS

Greg relies on nature's systems to raise his pigs, which are either purebred Duroc or 50 percent Duroc and 50 percent Berkshire. "I love the Durocs for their carcass uniformity," explains Greg. "The loins will all be the same, and the chefs like that. The color of the pork is amazing, the marbling is excellent."

He doesn't artificially inseminate his pigs, but instead breeds them naturally, letting the boars run with the females. "I never understood why I had to worry about it when the boars will," he says. "Nature is really good at setting up systems that work."

Once the pigs are pregnant, they are moved to a gestation pen—an area that is fenced off in the woods with covered steel huts to protect from the rain and elements. Two or three days before they're going to farrow, the pigs are moved to farrowing pens.

Each pen, which is about an acre in the woods, will have anywhere from four to 12 sows in the same pen. Each pregnant sow or gilt has a steel hut

filled with straw that is enclosed in colder months to give more protection from wind and rain.

"We farrow outside year round," Greg says, "though most of my sows and gilts are on a spring and fall farrowing. Pigs do fine farrowing outside, but it's a lot more work for us to take care of them, to keep them watered, make sure they have enough straw."

The males that are sold are separated off and put in their own fenced off area in the pasture to be fattened. The pigs spend their entire lives outdoors, between forest and pasture. In some parts of Greg's land, the woods are so thick you would barely know the pigs are there. Surprisingly, Greg says it isn't too hard to round them up.

Once Greg started selling his pigs to Charlie Trotter's, he quickly collected several other restaurant clients in Chicago. And along the way, everyone kept directing him to Rick Bayless at Frontera.

THE CHICKENS

"I tried my darnedest to sell my pork to Frontera," Greg says, "but they had a pig farmer in Wisconsin, and they were as loyal as could be."

Tracey Vowell, now running Three Sisters Garden (Chapter 14), was managing chef at Frontera and doing a lot of work with farms. "Tracey told me, 'Why don't you raise some chickens for me?'" Greg laughs. "That was another one of those wonderful moments where I said, 'Oh, that can't be that hard.'"

In 2000, the first year they started selling chickens to Rick Bayless, Gunthorp Farms went from producing 1,200 chickens to 12,000.

Every Thursday, Gunthorp Farms gets a delivery of day-old baby chicks that come in the mail. The chicks spend three to four weeks inside a warm brooding area, before they are moved out to pasture where they spend another five to six weeks.

Outdoors, the chickens have shelters that they run in and out of, pecking at the pasture and hunting for worms. There are 250 chickens per shelter, supplied with water and a feed of corn and soybeans that is ground on the farm.

"Most chickens are slaughtered under 40 days," Greg says. "Ours are closer to an average of seven or eight weeks, so the meat has had time to develop some flavor."

Today, Greg says they produce about 100,000 birds a year, including ducks and turkeys, which makes them one of the largest pastured chicken operations in the country.

THE PROCESSING

"It didn't take us long to realize that processing was our biggest challenge," says Greg, explaining that there are few USDA-certified plants to get animals processed, and few that have artisan butchers who cut for three-, four-, or five-start restaurants. In order to sell animals across state lines, they need to be USDA-certified.

Gunthorp Farms is one of the only farms in the country that has a USDA-inspected slaughter facility on site. It took 14 months after filling out the paperwork to even get the official to come visit the farm, and when you ask Greg how he finally managed to do it, he says with a smile, "I dragged them along the whole way, kickin' and screamin'."

Having a USDA-inspected processing plant means a few things. They are required to follow the same regulations as the big plants. They have a weekly meeting with an inspector, and there are at least two inspec-

Gunthorp sows farrow outside in the woods in one-acre-sized pens, with individual farrowing huts for as many as 12 pigs per pen.

tors at the plant during processing, one who stands on the line to inspect each animal and another who does all of the paperwork.

Greg says one of the ways his plant differs from most large-scale plants is that all of their processing is done by hand instead of machine.

"My concept is that you start with a clean healthy animal, and you keep it clean the whole time," Greg says. "We use an awful lot of water to keep the process clean, and we end up with a clean animal on the other end." The plant has continuous flowing water, and Greg says they use nearly twice the amount of water as larger plants, which he says tend to use chemicals instead to keep their animals clean.

Gunthorp butchers do "every cut imaginable" and fulfill specialty requests, like air chilling chickens for a few chefs (Greg says it helps retain more flavor than water chilling, which they do for most birds), or leaving the skin on the pigs, which is unusual because most processors skin them.

On an average week, they might process close to 1,600 chickens, 300 ducks, and 40 pigs. Slaughtering is done one day a week, on Monday. Greg says he won't process more than one day a week, because "there should be a little bit of quality of life in this. I don't think a person should be killing animals their whole week."

STRETCHING THE LIMITS

Greg never seems to be done pushing for the next thing, which right now is pastured rabbits.

"If I could figure out how we could do rabbits on the scale we could do chickens—if we could figure out a way to keep 'em in—I would rotationally graze rabbits," Greg's eyes get wide and his smile doesn't give away whether or not he is being serious.

He is. "Even the sustainable agriculture people think I'm nuts when I tell them I want to do that," he admits.

He just bought additional land down the road where he has put more of his pigs in the woods, and where he thinks he might be able to raise some heritage breeds of chicken. And his latest project is a new poured-

GET A TASTE OF GUNTHORP FARMS

BIG JONES
bigjoneschicago.com

FRONTERA GRILL
fronterakitchens.com

LULA CAFE
lulacafe.com

NIGHTWOOD
nightwoodrestaurant.com

ROOTSTOCK
rootstockbar.com

SEPIA
sepiachicago.com

cement smokehouse he built so that he can produce USDA-approved smoked bacon.

Greg is quick to credit chefs with the support that allows him to do what he loves; he's deeply appreciative of his clients, which include anywhere from 50 to 75 restaurants. "We're really fortunate," he says. "We have a clientele that appreciates what we're doing. If we didn't, our product and our whole process would be too expensive."

FROM THE FARMER: Greg Gunthorp

RESOURCES AND INSPIRATION

Magazine: *The Stockman Grass Farmer*

Website: **EatWild.com**

Writers: Michael Pollan, John Ikerd, Peter Drucker, Bill Heffernan, Michael Duffy, Alan Guebert, Temple Grandin

RECIPE

SLOW-ROASTED SHOULDER ROAST OR FRESH HAM ROAST

Lightly salt pork shoulder roast and place in a glass dish. Roast at 400°F (200°C) for 1 hour. Decrease the oven temperature to 200°F (90°C) or 225°F (110 °C), and roast for another 4 to 9 hours, depending on the size of roast. The internal temperature should be 170°F (80°C) in order to shred easily. Remove from the oven, let stand until cool enough to handle, and shred meat. Serve as is, or with your favorite barbecue sauce.

GUNTHORP FARMS FRIED CHICKEN

WITH POTATO-GOAT CHEESE PUREE, AND LEEKS, APPLES, AND GARLIC

By **Duncan Biddulph**, Rootstock

4 SERVINGS

> **8 chicken thighs**
> **Salt and black pepper**
> **1 cup (237 mL) cultured buttermilk**
> **1 teaspoon cayenne pepper**
> **1½ cups (182 g) all-purpose flour**
> **Vegetable oil or pork/duck fat for frying**
> **Potato-Goat Cheese Puree (recipe follows)**
> **Leeks, Apples, and Garlic (recipe follows)**

1. Season the thighs with 1 teaspoon salt per leg and a little black pepper. Let stand 1 hour.

2. Mix the buttermilk and cayenne pepper, and add the seasoned thighs. Refrigerate at least 4 hours, or as long as 24 hours. Remove the thighs from the buttermilk mixture. Wipe off and discard the excess buttermilk.

3. Combine the flour, 1 tablespoon salt and 1 teaspoon black pepper. Coat the thighs with the flour mixture, and let stand 30 minutes. Coat thighs again and fry them in hot fat for 6 to 9 minutes (duck or pork fat is best, but vegetable oil will do). Remove thighs from the oil to drain on a cooling rack or paper towels, and sprinke with salt while still sizzling.

4. To plate, place Potato-Goat Cheese Puree in the center of the serving plates. Arrange the chicken slightly off center on top of the puree, then spoon the Leeks, Apples, and Garlic around the outside of the plates.

POTATO-GOAT CHEESE PUREE

3 pounds (1.36 kg) yellow potatoes, such as Yukon gold, butterball, Dutch creamers

4 ounces (114 g) cream, plus extra as needed

2 ounces (57 g) unsalted butter

4 ounces (114 g) fresh goat cheese (chevre)

2 egg yolks (optional)

Salt, to taste

1. Peel the potatoes and cut into to rough chunks. Combine potatoes, cream, butter, and water to cover in a large saucepan and cook until tender. (Watch carefully to prevent boiling over.) Mash the potatoes with a wooden spoon, adding the goat cheese in stages. Stir in the egg yolks until well blended. Season to taste with salt.

2. For smoother mashed potatoes, pass the mashed potatoes through a mesh strainer, adding a little oil and some warm cream, if needed, to thin.

LEEKS, APPLES, AND GARLIC

1 or 2 leeks

2 apples, such as Northern Spy, Macintosh, or Pink Lady

2 ounces (57 g) unsalted butter

1 ounce (30 mL) water

1 tablespoon champagne vinegar

4 cloves whole garlic, peeled, thinly sliced

Salt and pepper

Additional butter

1 tablespoon chopped parsley

1. Trim the tops and roots of the leeks, cut into ¼-inch (6-mm) rounds to measure about 1½ cups (134 g), and wash in cold water to remove any sand. Drain and place on paper towels to absorb excess moisture. Cut the apples into ¼-inch (6-mm) cubes.

2. Heat butter, water and vinegar in a saucepan. When the mix begins to bubble, add the garlic and sweat for a few seconds. Add the leeks and stir 1 minute; add the apples, a pinch of salt and a couple cracks of pepper. Let the mixture cook down until the leeks are tender, but not mushy. Remove from the heat and stir in a small knob of butter and the parsley.

CHICKEN AND SAUSAGE JAMBALAYA

By **Paul Fehribach**, Big Jones

4–6 SERVINGS

"Going to Gunthorp Farms reminded me of being a kid and being on my Uncle Rich's farm, with pigs just wandering around, being happy. Ever since I grew up I always thought that is how pigs should live. It's always about the product, but when we start talking about animal product, it becomes more about the animals for me. It's a certain type of person who takes good care of their animals." –Paul Fehribach

1 (3½- to 4-pound [1.60- to 1.82-kg]) fresh whole chicken

Chicken Stock (recipe follows)

2 pounds (908 g) Andouille sausage, casing removed, chopped into ½- to ¾-inch [1.3- to 1.9-cm] pieces

1½ pounds (681 g) yellow onions, diced (½-inch [13-mm])

½ pound [227 g] green bell peppers, diced (½-inch [13-mm])

3 ribs celery, split lengthwise and chopped into ½-inch (13-mm) pieces

8 cloves garlic, crushed and chopped

4 tablespoons (18 g) Cajun seasoning

8 cups (1.52 kg) rice, such as American long grain or Louisiana popcorn rice, or any aromatic rice

4 tablespoons (59 mL) Worcestershire sauce

4 tablespoons (59 mL) Louisiana-Style hot sauce, such as Crystal, Louisiana, or Louisiana Gold

3 tablespoons (56 g) kosher salt, or more to taste

2 tablespoons pepper

1 teaspoon dried basil

1 teaspoon dried thyme

6 bay leaves

Sliced green onions

1. Remove the skin from the chicken. Remove excess fat from cavity and tail and reserve. Debone the chicken, reserving the bones for the Chicken Stock. Chop the chicken into 1-inch (2.5-cm) pieces and refrigerate until needed.

2. Prepare the Chicken Stock. This can take as long as 8 hours.

GUNTHORP FARMS

-- CUSTOM USDA INSPECTED POULTRY PROCESSING
-- WHOLESALE FREE RANGE PORK, CHICKEN, & DUCK
-- HOG ROASTING, CHIX BBQ, & CATERING

3. While the stock is cooking, render the sausage by placing the sausage on a rimmed baking sheet and bake at 350°F (180°C) until the sausage is a deep, dark rusty reddish-brown. Drain off the fat and reserve with the chicken fat until needed. Refrigerate the sausage until needed.

4. To prepare the jambalaya, heat a Dutch oven over high heat and heat the reserved rendered sausage fat until the first hint of smoke. (Watch carefully; you don't want to burn these volatile oils!) Add the onions and sauté, stirring constantly until onions are a light amber color. Add the bell peppers, celery, and garlic, and sauté until the bell peppers and celery begin to brown. Reduce heat to medium. Add the Cajun seasoning and sauté a few more minutes to release the oils in the spices and they brown slightly, turning the heat down gradually until it's off.

5. Add 2½ quarts (2.37 L) of the Chicken Stock, the rice, Worcestershire sauce, hot sauce, salt, black pepper, herbs, and the reserved chicken and sausage and stir just until mixed. Heat to a boil over medium heat. Occasionally, with a spatula, gently turn the rice mixture over to prevent scorching. (Do not to stir too much.)

6. Reduce the heat to medium-low, cover and continue to cook. At 3 minutes and again at 10 minutes, briefly lift the lid and with a spatula gently turn the rice to prevent sticking. Cook, covered, 20 minutes more without lifting the lid.

7. Peek under the lid and if there are still pools of liquid on top of the rice, replace the lid and continue cooking. (If there are only a few pools, check again in 3 minutes. If there's water over the entire surface of the rice, check again in 6 minutes.) When all the surface liquid has been absorbed, replace the lid, turn off the heat, and let stand for 30 minutes before serving. Taste and adjust seasoning, adding more salt, Cajun seasoning, or black pepper. Serve jambalaya topped with lots of sliced green onions.

(Continued on next page)

CHICKEN STOCK

Reserved chicken bones
1 onion, coarsely chopped
2 to 3 stalks celery, cut into chunks
Fresh herbs, such as parsley, thyme

1. Place bones in a Dutch oven and into the oven. Roast at 350°F (180°C) about 1 hour, or until bones are dark brown but not burned. Remove from the oven and place on the stovetop. Add cold water to cover bones by 1 inch (2.5 cm) . Heat to boiling over medium-high heat. Reduce to a simmer. Cook, skimming off foam, scum, and oil as it rises to the surface. Once scum formation slows, add onion, celery and herbs. Simmer at least 1 hour or up to 8 hours, skimming as needed. Strain and reserve stock until needed. Refrigerate stock if it won't be used within 1 hour.

GRILLED PORK PORTERHOUSE

WITH BUTTERMILK MASHED POTATOES, COLLARD GREENS, AND HAM HOCK

By **Andrew Zimmerman**, Sepia

4 SERVINGS

Basic Brine (recipe follows)
4 center-cut pork porterhouse (1 pound [454 g] each)
Buttermilk Mashed Potatoes (recipe follows)
Collard Greens and Ham Hock (recipe follows)
Sauce Charcuterie (recipe follows)
Salt and pepper

1. Prepare the Basic Brine. Chill completely.

2. Place pork chops in brine in non-reactive covered dish. Refrigerate 6 to 8 hours.

3. Remove the pork chops from the brine, dry them with paper towels, and allow them to come to room temperature. Meanwhile, prepare Buttermilk Mashed Potatoes, Collard Greens and Ham Hock, and Sauce Charcuterie. Prepare a charcoal grill for direct cooking or preheat a gas grill.

4. Lightly salt chops and grill them until they reach an internal temperature of 135°F (60°C), about 6 to 8 minutes.

5. Plate chops with collard greens, mashed potatoes, and top with sauce.

BASIC BRINE

1¼ gallons (4.75 L) cold water
¾ cup (225 g) kosher salt
½ cup (100 g) sugar
1 bay leaf
½ bunch fresh thyme
½ head garlic, cloves peeled
3 allspice berries
3 juniper berries

1. Combine all ingredients in a non-reactive stockpot. Heat to boiling, reduce heat, and simmer 10 minutes. Chill completely.

(Continued on next page)

BUTTERMILK MASHED POTATOES

1½ pounds (681 g) Yukon gold potatoes, unpeeled
3 tablespoons (45 mL) heavy cream, hot
3 tablespoons (45 mL) buttermilk, at room temperature
3 tablespoons (43 g) melted butter
Salt and white pepper

1. Place the potatoes in a large saucepan and cover them with about 2 inches (5 cm) of water. Heat to boiling, then simmer them until tender about 1 hour. Drain and peel the potatoes. Pass them through a food mill or ricer into a bowl. Stir in the cream, buttermilk, and butter. Season with salt and pepper. Cover and keep warm.

COLLARD GREENS AND HAM HOCK

3 tablespoons (43 g) bacon fat or butter
1 small onion, diced
2 cloves garlic, minced
1 bunch collard greens, stems removed, washed, cut into 1-inch (2.5-cm) pieces
½ smoked ham hock
3 quarts (2.85 L) water
Hot sauce, to taste
Salt and pepper, to taste

1. Melt the bacon fat in a large saucepan over medium heat. Add the onion and garlic and cook until tender. Add the collard greens, ham hock, and water. Simmer until greens are very tender and liquid is reduced by about two thirds. Pick the meat of the hocks and stir into greens. Season to taste with hot sauce, salt, and pepper. Keep warm.

SAUCE CHARCUTERIE

3 tablespoons (43 g) butter
⅔ cup (100 g) chopped shallots
⅔ cup (158 mL) white wine
2 cups (474 mL) veal stock
1½ tablespoons Dijon mustard

2 ounces (57 g) beurre manié (equal parts butter and flour kneaded together)
⅓ cup (50 g) cornichons, cut into strips or diced
Salt, to taste

1. Melt the butter in a medium saucepan over low heat. Add the shallots, cover, and sweat until tender. Add the wine, heat to a simmer, and reduce by half. Add stock, heat to a simmer, and simmer until the liquid is thick enough to coat the back of a spoon.

2. Whisk in some of the beurre manié, simmer until desired consistency is reached, adding more of the beurre manié, as needed. Strain, season to taste, and stir in the cornichons.

CHAPTER 4

HENRY'S FARM

Henry Brockman | Congerville, Illinois | henrysfarm.com

To get to the lower field on Henry's Farm, you take a steeply inclined gravel road through dense woods. When the road flattens out you come to a clearing, 10 acres of land surrounded on all sides by trees. Everything becomes quiet, calm, and at the same time, abuzz with life. In the early morning, the sun comes up behind the trees, gradually illuminating the entire field and drying the dew off of the ripening tomatoes, squash, beans, and lettuces.

Entering the field is like leaving the rest of the modern world behind. A few farmhands till the soil with push hoes, Henry walks the rows, taking notes in a worn notebook. As the sun gets higher in the sky and starts to warm the air, Henry pulls off his stocking hat and puts on a brimmed one with a neck flap. The day is fully underway.

If planting large fields of monoculture crops of corn and soy is like "covering a page with the same sentence over and over again," as Michael Pollan writes, what Henry Brockman is doing on his farm in central Illinois is more akin to what Shakespeare did with a page.

Biodiversity could sum up Henry's farm in a word. Last year he planted more than 650 varieties of vegetables: A total of 100 different types or categories—corn, beans, lettuces, tomatoes, potatoes, et cetera, et cetera—with different varieties of each.

"There are a lot of reasons to plant so many," Henry says, naming insurance through biodiversity (if one variety becomes susceptible to a pest or disease, another variety might be resistant), "but a big reason is that it's fun. For all of the other reasons, I probably wouldn't do it if it weren't fun."

AROUND THE WORLD AND BACK TO THE LAND

Before Henry was a farmer, before he returned to the land where he grew up, he traveled around the world, immersing himself in different cultures, countries, and cities, from Israel to Nepal to Japan. He collected languages along the way, and met his wife in Japan, where his first child was born.

Henry spent years abroad, but he was eventually drawn home. It was the place where he grew up with his five siblings, the farm where his parents grew and raised the food that fed their family.

"For me a big part of it was when our first child was born and we said, 'What are we going to feed this child?'" Henry says. "There was no way I was going to feed him the stuff I could buy in the store, so that left me with growing my own. I figured if I'm going to grow my own, why not do it for a living? I like to work outside, I like to be my own boss, I'm interested in the environment, and I kind of know how to do it because I grew up doing it."

Left: red and yellow chard growing on Henry's Farm. Above: garlic hangs to dry in the barn; Henry harvests bunches of purslane, a wild, nutrtious weed, for his Community Supported Agriculture (CSA) customers.

Henry's way of farming is an incredible amount of work. He takes no shortcuts, wastes little—be it an hour of the day or something from the farm, and has many high concepts about organic farming and agriculture that drive his methods.

"I consider what I do organic, even though I'm not certified organic," explains Henry. "I was certified for the first seven years, then I dropped out. Because it was one thing I didn't have to do in my life. I like the certification because there is a lot of false advertising going on, so in theory I think it's a great idea. But I feel like I've been in this long enough with the same customers at the same market—people know me and my farm."

Henry tries to be sustainable, and right now he's working on cutting down on use of gas, diesel, and electricity. He has an electric tractor and he hopes to convert a second tractor from gas. His market truck uses biodiesel made from used cooking oil, and it can get them all the way to the Evanston market and back, and to Bloomington and back for his Community Supported Agriculture (CSA) delivery—for a total of about 350 miles every week—supplemented by only 7 gallons of conventional diesel.

Henry also tries to minimize wasting water. In fact, he doesn't believe in irrigation, something that certainly sets him apart from other farmers in the Midwest; you will see no drip lines running the rows of his vegetables.

"Because I don't believe in irrigation, we have a very rudimentary system of watering," Henry says. "We should be able to grow vegetables in the Midwest without it; water is not necessarily a renewable resource."

Henry starts and transplants seedlings into the soil in the spring, so he only needs to transplant right before a rain to ensure the new plants will have enough water. If it's an especially dry spring and he needs to move his seedlings to the ground when there is no rain, he and his workers go through and dump buckets of water. The rest of the growing season, Henry starts from seed planted directly in the soil.

To encourage a healthy soil, Henry puts two 10-acre fields in a four-year rotation. He plants and grows vegetables for two years in one field, followed by two years of hay that lets the field lie fallow, or uncultivated. During that fallow time, he switches to growing vegetables in the other field. By raising clover and alfala during the fallow period, he is essentially growing fertilizer, crops that send nutrients into the soil, and will increase fertility once they are tilled in. While he is growing vegetables, as soon he is done with a bed for the season, he plants a high-protein cover crop with wheat that will survive the winter and eventually be tilled into the soil before he is ready to start planting again in the spring.

"I haven't increased my acreage for the past 15 years, but I've been able to grow more every year," he adds. "That is the experience and knowledge gained over those years."

A farm hand uses a push hoe, a gentle way of agitating the soil for weeding or preparing the rows.

THE CHEFS

Ten years ago, Henry's first restaurant client was Blackbird, with sous chef Brian Wolff coming to shop at the farmers' market in Evanston. "He made an effort to come to the market every week and shop," says Henry, who credits Wolff with his relationship with Blackbird that lasted for many years through several different sous chefs, including Jared Van Camp. His current connection with The Publican's Brian Huston—who shops at the market weekly—also comes from Wolff, as they were at Blackbird together.

Henry has decided not to deliver to restaurants and to put his time and resources instead toward the farm and his one market day. If chefs want Henry's produce, they have to go to him in Evanston and shop just like everyone else. Only a few are willing to go to Evanston every Saturday morning and hand-pick their produce from Henry's farm stand, because so many rely on delivery or pick-up at Green City Market.

"One of the main chefs now is Carlos Ysaguirre," says Henry, referring to the chef of Acre and Anteprima, restaurants in Chicago's Andersonville neighborhood. "He is wonderful; he does it the way it really should be done. He doesn't come with a list, he comes and sees what I have. He has a really good eye and buys whatever is good that week, rather than what his menu needs."

THE MARKET

On a chilly market day in early May, the thermometer had dropped from 80 degrees two days prior to a chilling 45 degrees. It was the second Evanston market of the season, and Henry didn't think it would be too crowded. At just after 7 am, right when the market opens, he was right and the market wasn't very busy. But there was an energetic and growing crowd around one farmer's stall: Henry's.

It's no surprise that Henry has such loyal fans, as he's been a market fixture for 19 of the Evanston market's 36 years. It's not surprising that he's become a local superhero in the community: Once his customers understand the degree of care and hard work that goes into every bundle of arugula or handful of Jerusalem artichokes, once they taste his potatoes and cook with his onions, they never want to go back, and they want to continue to support the farmer who supplies their family with this food.

Henry darts around his stand, refilling empty wooden crates, restacking shopping baskets, and greeting familiar customers. He doesn't skip a beat while he tallies produce in his head.

It's hard to put a finger on what Henry does best, but some things standout simply by the number of varieties. "I'm known for what I call my amazing wall of lettuce, there are 50 types of lettuces," Henry says. "It's a huge display, three boxes high, six, seven, eight, or nine tables full of it. I also have a lot of heirloom tomatoes. I'm known for all of my greens. Not many people have as many as I do." He pauses. "And then, I am basically known for having, well, everything."

Henry laughs softly. "If you need something, you can probably get it from me."

GET A TASTE OF HENRY'S FARM

ACRE
acrerestaurant.com

ANTEPRIMA
anteprimachicago.net

THE PUBLICAN
thepublicanrestaurant.com

FROM THE FARMER: Henry Brockman

RESOURCES AND INSPIRATION

The Land Connection is a not-for-profit based in central Illinois founded by my sister, Terra Brockman, that helps connect the growers of organic food to the eaters of organic food. It is also active in training new organic farmers.

Growing for Market is a monthly journal for small-scale fruit, vegetable, flower, and livestock growers. I learn something new with every issue.

RECIPE

HIROKO'S KIMPIRA GOBO
(Stir-Fried Burdock and Carrots with Sesame and Soy Sauce)

> 2 cups (236 g) prepared burdock*
> 2 cups (256 g) prepared carrots*
> 2 tablespoons sesame oil
> 1 tablespoons vegetable oil
> 1 tablespoon soy sauce
> 2 teaspoons dashi (dried fish stock) (optional)
> 1 tablespoon water (optional)
> 1 tablespoon toasted sesame seeds, for garnish

To prepare the burdock and carrots, wash them and scrape them with the back of a knife (they don't need to be peeled). Cut them into matchstick-size pieces. As you cut the burdock, put the pieces in a bowl of cold water to prevent them from browning.

1. Heat the oils in a large saucepan over medium-high heat. Add the drained burdock and carrots and stir-fry about 5 to 7 minutes. (The burdock will change from milky-white to a shiny gray/brown.) Add soy sauce and continue stir-frying. Add the dashi dissolved in the water, if desired. Continue stir-frying until all the liquid has evaporated. Remove from heat and transfer to serving dish. Sprinkle toasted sesame seeds on top.

HENRY'S LEEKS, FRENCH FINGERLING POTATOES, AND WARM SOFT-BOILED EGGS

By **Jared Van Camp**, Old Town Social and Nellcôte

4 SERVINGS

"Henry Brockman is not a normal farmer. He's not a normal person. The man works harder than any human being I have ever met and his passion for farming (more importantly farming the right way) cannot be equaled. The vegetables and fruits he grows reap the benefits of this passion. Henry and I have had legitimately lengthy conversations about single varieties of lettuce. His knowledge is nothing short of amazing. And Henry has taught me one of the most valuable lessons that every chef needs to know: Food that tastes better is better for you."—Jared Van Camp

> 3 tablespoons (45 mL) red wine vinegar
> 4 cornichons, finely chopped
> 1 shallot, finely minced
> 2 teaspoons Creole mustard
> ¼ cup (59 mL) extra-virgin olive oil
> 2 quarts (1.90 L) plus 1 quart (948 mL) water, divided
> 4 eggs
> 8 small leeks (about ½ inch [13 cm] in diameter)
> 1 pound (454 g) small French Fingerling potatoes
> ¼ cup (12 g) finely sliced garlic chives
> Salt and pepper, to taste

1. To prepare the vinaigrette, combine the vinegar, cornichons, shallot, and mustard in a bowl. Slowly whisk in the olive oil. Reserve.

2. Prepare an ice bath. Heat 2 quarts (1.90 L) of water to boiling. Gently place the eggs in the boiling water. Cook exactly 5 minutes. Transfer the eggs and to the ice bath. After 15 minutes, remove and peel the eggs, being careful not to damage the fragile whites. Reserve.

3. Trim off the root end and all the dark green parts from the leeks. Cook the leeks about 6 to 7 minutes in boiling salted water just until tender. (They should not be slimy.) Remove the leeks from the water to a shallow dish and pour

half the vinaigrette over them while they are still warm. Cool and cut them into 1-inch (2.5-cm) sections. Reserve.

4. Place the potatoes in cold salted water in a saucepan, heat to boiling, reduce heat, and simmer until tender, about 20 minutes. Drain and slice the potatoes into ½-inch (13-mm) slices. Pour the remaining vinaigrette over the potatoes while they are still warm. Reserve.

5. Heat the remaining 1 quart (948 mL) of water to simmering. Remove it from the heat and place the 4 reserved, chilled and peeled eggs into the hot water. Cover and let stand 5 minutes.

6. While the eggs are warming, gently toss the leeks, potatoes, and garlic chives together in a bowl. Season to taste with salt and pepper. Divide the vegetable mixture among 4 plates. Place one egg on each plate. Season each egg with a little salt and black pepper. Serve immediately.

STUFFED SUMMER ZUCCHINI AND FRIED EGG WITH TOMATILLO SALSA

By **Carlos Ysaguirre**, Acre and Anteprima

"At the restaurant, I make an effort to stock our cooler with Henry's vegetables. I believe the customer that walks through our front doors deserves the best the Midwest has to offer. His harvest is immaculate, year in, year out. This recipe is designed to feature several of Henry's treasures during the peak of summer."—Carlos Ysaguirre, Acre and Anteprima

> 2 zucchini (8 to 10 inches [20 to 25 cm] long, 2 to 3 inches [5 to 7.5 cm] in diameter)
>
> Olive oil
>
> Salt and pepper
>
> 2 small poblano chili peppers, roasted, peeled, cut into thin strips
>
> 1 cup (160 g) sweet corn kernels cut from the cob
>
> ½ pound (227 g) baby spinach
>
> 1 cup (227 g) queso fresco
>
> 1 bunch cilantro, chopped
>
> Tomatillo Salsa (recipe follows)
>
> 2 egg whites
>
> ½ cup (61 g) all-purpose flour
>
> 6 farm-fresh eggs
>
> Additional queso fresco and chopped cilantro, for garnish

1. Cut 1 zucchini crosswise into 4 (2-inch [5-cm]) cylinders. Dice the remaining zucchini (about 1 cup [124 g]).

2. Lightly oil the 4 zucchini cylinders and season with salt and pepper. Roast in a shallow baking pan at 375°F (190°C) 15 minutes. Remove from oven and cool.

3. While the zucchini is roasting, sauté the diced zucchini in a large skillet over medium heat until crisp-tender. Add to the bowl of poblano peppers. Quickly sauté the corn in the same skillet. Add the spinach and sauté just until wilted. Add corn mixture to peppers. Cool. Stir in queso fresco and cilantro. Season to taste with salt and pepper.

4. Prepare the Tomatillo Sauce. Keep warm.

5. Whip the egg whites until stiff but not dry.

6. When the zucchini is cool enough to handle, hollow out ¾ of the cylinders. Fill to the top with the poblano pepper mixture. Dredge the cylinders in flour and dip them into the whipped egg whites.

7. Heat olive oil in a large skillet, and pan-fry the stuffed zucchini, turning until all sides are golden brown. Drain on paper towels. Remove all but 2 tablespoons of the oil from skillet.

8. Fry the eggs sunny side up, in batches if necessary.

9. To serve ladle 2 to 3 tablespoons of the tomatillo salsa onto each of the serving plates. Place stuffed zucchini cylinders on top of the sauce. Top each of the stuffed zucchini with the fried egg. Garnish with any extra cheese or cilantro.

TOMATILLO SALSA

½ pound (227 g) tomatillos, husks removed
1 medium-sized Spanish onion, diced
1 small clove garlic
Juice of 1 lime, to taste
Salt and pepper, to taste

1. Combine tomatillos, onion and garlic in a medium saucepan and add just enough water to cover the vegetables. Heat to a slow simmer and cook until vegetables are soft enough to blend, about 20 minutes. Drain the ingredients and process in a food processor or blender to desired consistency. Season to taste with lime juice, salt and pepper.

SUNCHOKES WITH KNOB ONIONS AND ROMESCO

By **Paul Kahan and Brian Huston**, The Publican

4–6 SERVINGS

> Romesco (recipe follows)
> 3 pounds (1.36 kg) sunchokes
> 1 pound (454 g) knob onions
> Olive oil
> Juice of ½ lemon
> Salt and pepper
> 1 bunch parsley, chopped

1. Prepare Romesco.

2. Leaving the skins on, scrub sunchokes to remove all dirt. Cut sunchokes into about 1-inch (2.5-cm) cubes. Peel the onions. Depending on the size of the onions, cut them into halves or quarters to match the size of the cubed sunchokes.

3. Sauté the sunchokes and onions, in batches if necessary, in oil in a large ovenproof skillet 1 minute. Roast them in a 400°F (200°C) oven until the sunchokes are tender, 5 to 8 minutes. Remove from oven and season to taste with the lemon juice, salt, and pepper. Top with parsley and serve over Romesco.

ROMESCO

> 6 tomatoes
> 6 red bell peppers
> 1½ slices bread
> 1 cup (237 mL) extra-virgin olive oil
> 3 fresno chili peppers
> 1 dried, smoked ancho chili
> 1 head garlic
> ½ cup (72 g) almonds
> ¼ cup (36 g) hazelnuts
> Sherry vinegar
> Salt and pepper

1. Cut the tomatoes in half and place them in a shallow baking pan. Roast at 400°F (200°C) 30 minutes.

2. While the tomatoes are roasting, blister the skins of the bell peppers over the flames a gas burner or on a grill. Transfer the peppers to a plastic bag and close the bag, or to a bowl and cover with plastic wrap, 15 minutes. Peel skins and remove seeds.

3. Fry the bread in oil in a large skillet until crispy.

4. Place all the ingredients in a food processor and process until course paste, adding the rest of the olive oil as the mixture processes.

CHAPTER 5

KILGUS FARMSTEAD

Matt and Paul Kilgus | Fairbury, Illinois | kilgusfarmstead.com

PLEASANT MEADOWS FARM

Justin and Trent Kilgus | Fairbury, Illinois

W hen the Kilgus family heard that Rick Bayless was looking for a local farm to supply his Chicago restaurants with milk and cream, they started to think about a change in their dairy business.

In 2006, Matt and Paul Kilgus were selling their milk to a large milk co-op, and it was becoming a struggle to support their families on 90 cows. They began to consider farmstead milk, bottling their own product and creating a niche market for themselves.

"We felt our hands were tied," Matt says. "We thought this might be a good opportunity to control our market a little more, and to create more income for more family members to come back to the farm."

They visited farms in Iowa, Indiana, and Wisconsin, and talked to out-of-state dairies that were bottling their own milk. The more they looked into it they realized that no other dairy in the state of Illinois was selling farmstead milk at that time.

In 2009 they started bottling their own milk, and Kilgus Dairy became Kilgus Farmstead.

FARMSTEAD MILK

Matt's grandfather started the dairy farm in the 1950s with a small herd of Holstein cows, which his dad and his uncle Paul eventually took over. When his dad passed away more than a decade ago, Matt went into partnership with Paul.

The family gradually switched over to Jersey cows in the '90s. Jerseys are smaller than the black-and-white Holsteins, and they produce less milk. But the milk they do give is incredibly rich in flavor and high in protein. They changed 50 acres of corn and soybeans over to a series of two-and-a-half-acre paddocks of rye grass, orchard grass, and clover, for grazing. Every 24 hours, the cows move to a fresh paddock of grass so that it has time to grow back.

The Kilguses say the change to pasturing their cows has improved their operation immensely. They have a healthier herd that spends the days outside; plus the cows harvest their own food and re-fertilize the pasture by spreading their waste across the field.

But the biggest change to their operation was the decision to bottle their own milk. When they set out to do it, they realized how rare it was for a dairy farm to do farmstead milk. "We were the first to do it in Illinois," Matt says, "but it's a trend that is becoming more popular."

Along with positive reception came some confusion from consumers. "People hadn't seen farmstead milk before and misunderstood, thinking it was raw milk," Matt explains. "But it's not—we're a Grade-A bottling plant, just on a small scale."

One of the unusual aspects of farmstead milk is that it is single source, meaning the milk only comes from the cows on that farm. A large dairy co-op often buys milk from hundreds of dairies across the state and mixes it. Matt says it is a nice marketing point. "We can say, 'Hey this is just the milk from our cows,'" he says. "But of course it can work both ways too—you have to make sure the quality is there."

PASTEURIZATION AND HOMOGENIZING

When the Kilgus family began bottling their own milk, they had to decide how they would pasteurize. Vat pasteurization holds the milk at 145°F (63°C) for 30 minutes. Ultra pasteurized milk, common in organic milks with an especially long shelf life, is held above 200°F (93°C) for 15 seconds.

The Kilgus family raises the male cattle for meat, which they sell at their farm store.

"There's not much to that milk once it's zapped at such high temps," Matt says. "We're the midrange—we hold our milk at 164°F (73°C) for a minimum of 15 seconds." With the temperature and time they settled on, their milk retains a less-cooked taste and they can move milk through their operation at a more efficient pace.

Another decision was whether or not to homogenize. Homogenization breaks milk's fat particles into a uniform size that resists separating and rising. Non-homogenized milk needs to be agitated often so that the cream mixes in.

"We knew we had to make a different product, so we decided not to," Matt says. "It was one less step, and keeps it more natural."

But of course, with non-homogenized farmstead milk, there was yet another learning curve for consumers.

"We were placing this product in conventional stores with a cream line and we started getting returns that said 'bad milk,'" Matt says. "So we try to get out there, demo the milk, and tell the story."

Above: Kilgus cows spend most of the day grazing in the fields, and are brought in twice a day for milkings. Right: The milking facility awaits the Jersey cows, visibily ready for their second milking of the day.

One of the times they were out their telling their story at a Whole Foods in Chicago, one of the head financial guys of Intelligentsia, the upscale Chicago-based coffee company focused on brewing high quality, single-cup coffee, happened to be there and said, "This is just what we're looking for." The Kilguses were amazed by their luck. Soon Kilgus milk was in every Intelligentsia store in the city, and from that point forward, Matt and Paul could relax a little. Restaurant sales started to increase, and Kilgus started selling to places like Sandra Holl's Floriole Bakery in Lincoln Park, Hopleaf, Nightwood, MK, and Big Jones. A handful of other restaurants with chefs happy to find a local milk source soon followed.

"When we started, we went from 0 to 600 gallons a week in sales; now we're between 3,000 and 3,500 a week," says Matt, almost surprised by it himself. "Which is capacity."

PLEASANT MEADOWS FARM

By the time Kilgus milk was in production, a few years had passed since the team at Frontera had been clamoring for local milk and cream, and in that time, they had found someone else to supply them. Initially the Kilguses were disappointed but understood that Frontera being loyal to its farmers was a good thing for the family: "Once they find something they like, they don't switch. Which is good for Justin and Trent, because they use their goats for meat."

Justin and Trent are Paul's two boys, and Marty Travis at Spence Farm helped to connect them to Chicago chefs. They were both still in high school when they applied for a Frontera Farmer Foundation grant, got it, and began raising and selling goats to Frontera restaurants.

Justin and Trent got their first goat as a pet, and as Justin says, "We really didn't think it would turn into something like this."

They raise heritage Boer goats, known for flavorful meat and yearlong breeding. The goats breed naturally and are raised on pasture throughout the year. "We feed them a corn-based diet, as opposed to just letting them out on grass," Justin says. "It gives them a little more marbling, more flavor to the meat, and is what sets us apart from other producers. It's a lot more expensive to feed them, but it is a higher quality and flavor."

When Stephanie Izard was in the process of opening her West Loop restaurant, Girl and the Goat, she was looking for the best tasting goat she could find. "The goat is awesome, it's delicious," she says. "It's a very clean taste, rich and a bit fattier than other goat. We serve the loins medium-rare, we do carpaccio, sausage, smoked and pulled goat, whole goat legs—basically anything you can do with goat."

Girl and the Goat orders directly through them, placing orders every Monday. The goats are processed Tuesday, then hang for a couple of days to air out before

GET A TASTE OF KILGUS FARMSTEAD...

BIG JONES
bigjoneschicago.com

FLORIOLE
floriole.com

HOPLEAF
hopleaf.com

MK
mkchicago.com

NIGHTWOOD
nightwoodrestaurant.com

...AND PLEASANT MEADOWS FARM

GIRL AND THE GOAT
thegirlandthegoat.com

FRONTERA GRILL
fronteragrill.com

they are vacuumed packed and driven up to Chicago Friday morning to be delivered. Justin and Trent sell everything fresh. And because Boer goats breed year round, they are able to process and sell their goats in all four seasons.

"That was Stephanie's main concern when she came down to the farm: 'Right now you're selling two or there goats a week; are you going to be able to sell 12 or 13 goats a week and be consistent?'"

Soon after they got started, an old farmstead came up down the road. Once they got the Girl and the Goat account, the Kilgus brothers bought the place and grew their herd.

"It was a big commitment, maybe 500 goats a year or more than what we were doing before. Once we picked up Stephanie Izard, it took us to the next level," Justin says. "Frontera helped us get started, and Girl and the Goat brought us to where we are today."

FROM THE FARMERS: The Kilgus Family

RECIPE

BAKED POTATO SOUP

6–8 SERVINGS

1 pound (454 g) bacon
⅔ cup (152 g) unsalted butter
⅔ cup (80 g) all-purpose flour
7 cups (1.66 L) whole milk
4 large potatoes, baked and cubed
4 green onions, chopped
2 cups (228 g) shredded cheddar cheese
1 cup (237 mL) sour cream
Salt and pepper, to taste
Additional shredded cheddar cheese, for garnish
Additional chopped green onions, for garnish

1. Cook the bacon until crisp. Drain on paper towels and crumble. Reserve some of the bacon for garnish.

2. Melt the butter in a large saucepan over medium heat. Add the flour and cook until slightly bubbly. Whisk in the milk. Increase the heat and add the potatoes and green onions. Heat until the mixture begins to thicken. (Do not boil.)

3. Cook 10 minutes. Add the cheese, sour cream, and bacon, stirring until the cheese is melted. Season to taste with the salt and pepper. Garnish with the additional cheese, the green onions and the reserved bacon.

From left to right: Paul, Justin, Trent, and Matt Kilgus.

GOAT CHORIZO AND FRESH RICOTTA

By **Stephanie Izard**, Girl and the Goat

"At the restaurant, we serve both on flatbread drizzled with a little creamy oregano vinaigrette."—Stephanie Izard

> 3½ pounds (1.59 kg) Pleasant Meadows goat
> 14 ounces (397 g) pork
> 6½ ounces (184 g) fatback
> 3 ounces (85 g) beef fat
> 2 ounces (57 g) Chorizo Spice Mix (recipe follows)
> 1 ounce (28 g) salt
> ¾ tablespoon dried oregano
> ½ tablespoon dried rosemary
> ½ teaspoon dried thyme
> ½ (14 g) ounce garlic cloves
> 5 ounces (130 mL) beef stock
> 4 tablespoons (59 mL) red wine vinegar
> 1½ tablespoons tequila
> Canola oil
> Fresh Ricotta (recipe follows)

1. Cut the goat, pork, and fats into 1-inch (2.5-cm) cubes. Place in a baking pan and freeze until partially frozen (not fully frozen, but definitely very cold). Toss the meat with the spice mix. Then grind the meat mixture in a cold meat grinder with a slightly larger die.

2. Return the meat mixture to the freezer. When partially frozen, remove and grind with a slightly smaller die. Alternate grinding meat with oregano, rosemary, thyme, and garlic cloves.

3. Put the meat mixture into a cold mixing bowl of a stand mixer fitted with a paddle attachment. Begin mixing on slow then increase to medium speed when the meat begins to emulsify. Add the beef stock, red wine vinegar, and tequila. Continue to mix until the meat begins to become sticky.

4. To cook off meat, heat a small amount of canola oil in a skillet over medium-high heat. Add the meat mixture, in batches, and cook until cooked through, breaking up with a wooden spoon. Remove the chorizo from skillet, save the fat, and drain the chorizo on paper towels until ready to use.

CHORIZO SPICE MIX

 2 ounces (57 g) dried guajillo chili peppers
 ⅓ ounce (9 g) dried ancho chili peppers
 ⅛ ounce (5.6 g) chili de arbor
 ½ ounce (14 g) smoked paprika
 1 teaspoon ground cumin
 1 teaspoon ground coriander
 ⅓ teaspoon ground cinnamon
 ¼ teaspoon ground dried ginger
 Pinch ground nutmeg

1. Process all ingredients in a food processor until finely ground.

FRESH RICOTTA

 1 gallon (3.80 L) whole milk from Kilgus
 ⅓ to ½ cup (79 to 119 mL) distilled white vinegar
 ½ tablespoon salt

1. Heat milk to 184°F (84°C). While gently stirring, slowly drizzle vinegar into milk until it breaks. Let stand 1 hour. Strain and stir in salt.

CREAMY OREGANO VINAIGRETTE

 1 cup (30 g) oregano leaves
 ⅓ cup (10 g) cilantro leaves
 ⅓ cup (79 mL) sherry vinegar
 2½ tablespoons (38 mL) honey
 2½ tablespoons (38 mL) lemon juice
 ½ cup (119 mL) extra-virgin olive oil
 ½ cup (119 mL) rice bran oil

 Salt, to taste

1. Combine all the ingredients, except the salt, in a food processor or blender and process until desired consistency is reached. Season to taste with salt.

PAWPAW PANNA COTTA*

By **Paul Fehribach**, Big Jones

12 (3-OUNCE [85-G]) SERVINGS

"I used to drink milk from my Uncle Lee's dairy farm growing up. After moving away and becoming a chef, I hated milk until I found Kilgus, which is minimally processed. The Jersey cows make really great milk." –Paul Fehribach

2 tablespoons powdered unflavored gelatin

½ cup (119 mL) water

3 cups (711 mL) heavy cream

1 cup (200 g) sugar

1 tablespoon vanilla extract

1 teaspoon salt

4 cups (600 g) fresh pawpaw pulp* (about 6 large or 8 small), pitted, strained through a fine mesh tamis (cloth strainer)

You can substitute mashed banana, or cooked mashed pumpkin or sweet potato

1. Sprinkle the gelatin on top of the water and let stand 3 to 5 minutes or until softened.

2. Meanwhile, place 12 (3-ounce [90-mL]) molds, such as cups, ramekins, or small soufflé cups, in the refrigerator to chill.

3. Place the cream, sugar, vanilla, and salt in a non-reactive saucepan and heat to boiling over medium heat. Add dissolved gelatin to the cream mixture and return to boiling, whisking constantly. Immediately, remove from the heat, whisk in the pawpaw pulp, and quickly ladle into the chilled molds. Refrigerate until set, about 4 hours.

4. When panna cotta is set, cover the molds with plastic wrap and refrigerate until needed, up to 1 week.

5. To unmold, quickly dip each mold into hot water for 15 seconds, then run a thin spatula around the edge, and invert panna cotta onto a plate.

MICK KLUG FARM

Mick and Abby Klug | St. Joseph, Michigan | mickklugfarm.com

Abby Klug's grandparents—Mick Klug's parents—started their family farm in St. Joseph, Michigan, more than 80 years ago by wholesaling their fruit at the Benton Harbor Fruit Market. When Mick purchased the farm from them 50 years later, he continued to grow the varieties of peaches, seedless grapes, and plums, as well as sweet and sour cherries, apples, and red and black raspberries his parents had grown on the farm. For a while, searching for his farming niche, Mick grew yellow squash and zucchini to sell at the same wholesale market.

"All of farming is risky, but when you are wholesaling, it all depends on the market," says Abby, Mick's younger daughter who works fulltime on the farm with him. "Some years, my dad would get $2 for a bushel box of zucchini."

It didn't take long for Mick to realize he needed to figure out another way to make a living.

"Nineteen eighty was when Chicago started its farmers' market, and it didn't have enough farmers," Mick says. "Our neighbor called and said, 'They're looking for more growers, you should go.' That's how I got started with the Lincoln Park Market, which was like what Green City is now."

Mick sent Abby's aunt and uncle at first, to sell a few boxes of what they were growing. It started off slowly, but it didn't take long before things picked up, and people grew interested in buying local produce. "It was actually Rick Bayless who started going to the market and buying stuff from my dad," Abby says. "Rick said, 'I would buy a lot more from you if you would deliver it to my restaurant,' and my dad said, 'I can do that.' He would do anything, you know?"

WORKING WITH CHEFS

Frontera has been a customer since the beginning. Shaw's Crab House was another early buyer. And in recent years, a lot of business has come from smaller spots like The Bristol, Lula, and Nightwood, from chefs who are committed to using local ingredients, Abby says. They also sell to Spiaggia, the Hilton Hotels, as well as the Hyatts, and a long list of other restaurants throughout the city.

One of Abby's first tasks when she started working fulltime on the farm a couple of years ago was to create a regular email list. Now Mick Klug Farm sends out two emails a week to a list of 100 Chicago chefs. The email lists what they have available that week for what price, and allows them to email in their order.

"That has increased the restaurant business a lot," Abby says. "It makes it really easy for them, so they're not trying to get a hold of my dad to try to figure out what we have and what the prices are.

"Although Shaw's still calls, Frontera still calls—they don't care about the email, they want to talk to my dad," she adds, laughing.

ORGANIC: TO BE OR NOT TO BE

Abby and Mick work on growing their crops in a way that minimizes pesticide use. They plant cover crops between the rows of perennials to increase nutrient-rich green manure in order to minimize fertilizer use, and have a field scout who tracks threatening diseases and pests in the farm's plants.

Growing fruit one hundred percent organically in southwestern Michigan is notoriously hard and nearly impossible, because of the high humidity and moisture, which causes rot and mildew, and attracts pests.

Mick and Abby say they use organic materials to deter these problems, but even the decision to do that isn't as straightforward as it seems.

Organic has been made especially popular by the media, and by magazines touting "the dirty dozen"—a list of 12 fruits and vegetables that come with the claim they should always be bought organic. But being certified organic isn't the final word, according to some farmers, like Mick and Abby.

Raspberries are ready to be picked; grapes are still ripeneing on the vine; Abby and Mick stop working for a second to smile.

Pesticides are rated at three levels: *caution*, *warning*, and *danger*. Certified organic fruit growers are permitted to use a variety of pesticides, some of which are at the *warning*, or level two, rating.

Though the goal of Mick Klug Farm is to use only materials rated at the *caution* level—in other words, a lower-level toxicity than some of the inputs allowed for organic growing—they find there are customers who still only seek out organics.

"It can be really frustrating," Abby says, "because we are trying our best, and there are people looking only for organic fruit, but they don't know all the details."

"We really want to be safe, we want to protect the environment, protect people, and generally just do the right thing," says Abby, who is currently working with her dad to get third party certification from Food Alliance, an organization that promotes land stewardship, humane animal treatment, and fair working conditions.

THE FRUIT

If there is one thing that might convince someone instantly that just-picked, locally grown, heirloom varieties of fruits and vegetables are superior in flavor to those sitting in the produce aisle at the store, it has to be Mick Klug grapes.

Abby said it's a recent customer obsession: "Before it was like, 'Mick Klug's peaches are unbelievable'— which they still are—but now people are obsessed with the seedless grapes."

Canadice, Niagara, Jupiter, Neptune—each seedless variety has a different, unbelievably delicious tangy, floral, or fruity flavor. It's easy to see how market customers get fanatical; any of these grapes is sure to spoil its eater forever.

Mick Klug Farm has a consistent and loyal restaurant clientele, seven weekly markets in Chicago, and a Community Supported Agriculture (CSA) program

GET A TASTE OF MICK KLUG FARM

ACRE
acrerestaurant.com

ANTEPRIMA
anteprimachicago.com

CARNIVALE
carnivalechicago.com

FRONTERA
fronterakitchens.com

LULA CAFE
lulacafe.com

NIGHTWOOD
nightwoodrestaurant.com

PERENNIAL VIRANT
perennialchicago.com

SHAW'S CRAB HOUSE
shawscrabhouse.com

VIE
vierestaurant.com

Mick recently started growing sweet corn, which he harvests early when its size is small and the flavor is concentrated.

that supplies members with weekly fruit and vegetables. Despite all of the directions they are going, and the large varieties and quantities of fruit they are growing on more than 100 acres of land, the quality of product is consistent and strong. Abby attributes this to the workers they hire to help farm their land—a team of as many 15 workers who also live on the farm.

"A lot of vegetable farmers can pay their guys by the unit, but we pay by the hour," Abby explains, "because we want them to only pick the best berries on the bush as opposed to a certain quantity. If you pay by the hour, they'll pick the best fruit."

It is still a challenge, especially with peaches, to get it just right.

"People want it ripe, ready to eat, but they don't want it to have a bruise on it—they want the best of both worlds!" Abby laughs. "If you pick a peach ripe and ready to eat, it's going to have a bruise on it by the time it gets to Chicago, and then you can't sell it."

Somehow all during peach season, Mick and Abby seem to figure out the best of both worlds.

For the fruit that does quickly over-ripen or bruise, Abby says the recent trend of jamming and preserving by chefs has helped. Chicago chef Jared

Van Camp of Old Town Social and Nellcôte makes what he calls a "bachelor's jam." Made of cherries, peaches, and berries from the farm, and a large amount of rum, the jam is poured into an old bourbon barrel and left to develop boozy, fruity flavors, to be served warm in the winter once summer and fall fruit harvests are long gone.

THE FUTURE

Although Abby moved to Chicago after she graduated from Michigan State, she found herself always returning to her family's farm in the summer. Farming was second nature to her, to the point where she hadn't actually considered this endeavor in her backyard as a career option. It took her a few years working, going to graduate school, and working some more, to realize that she wanted to return to the farm full-time. Though she is only in her late twenties and Mick still runs the farm, she plans to eventually take over, when her dad gets to the age where he can't do all of the work.

She says the main challenge will be the physical side of farming. With her slight build she can drive a tractor, but she can't do a lot of the physical labor that's required, and might have to someday hire a foreman to help do what her dad does now. She seems committed and happy with her decision to move back to the farm.

"We'll see, but I think I'm stuck now," she says, laughing. "I'm just gonna do it!"

FROM THE FARMER: Mick Klug

RESOURCES AND INSPIRATION

The documentary about local foods, *Ingredients*.

Michigan State University Extension Center is the best resource—we couldn't farm without their help.

The **Michigan Agriculture Environmental Assurance Program** is an innovative, proactive program that helps farms voluntarily prevent or minimize agricultural pollution risks.

RECIPE

GRANDMA KLUG'S PEACH COBBLER

6–8 SERVINGS

8 to 10 cups (1.2 to 1.5 kg) sliced peeled fresh peaches
1 teaspoon ground cinnamon
¼ teaspoon ground nutmeg
1 cup (227 g) unsalted butter, softened
2 cups (400 g) plus ½ cup (100 g) sugar, divided
2 cups (242 g) all-purpose flour
2 teaspoons baking powder
½ teaspoon salt
1 cup (237 mL) milk
2 teaspoons vanilla extract

1. Preheat the oven to 350°F (180°C).

2. Place the peaches in a 13 × 9-inch (32.5 × 22.5-cm) baking dish. Sprinkle the peaches evenly with cinnamon and nutmeg.

3. Cream the butter and 2 cups (400 g) of the sugar in the large bowl of an electric mixer. Add the combined flour, baking powder, and salt alternately with the combined milk and vanilla, beating well after each addition.

4. Spoon the batter evenly over the peaches. Sprinkle with the remaining ½ cup (100 g) of sugar. Bake about 1 hour or until the peaches are bubbly and the topping is lightly browned. Serve warm.

RED WINE POACHED BOSC PEARS AND GOAT CHEESE

By **Carlos Ysaguirre**, Acre and Anteprima

4 SERVINGS

"At the restaurant we pride ourselves on seeking out the finest ingredients, and Mick Klug never lets us down. Simple recipes require pristine ingredients for maximum flavor."—Carlos Ysaguirre

4 evenly sized bosc pears
4 cups (948 mL) red wine
1 cup (237 mL) honey
1 cup (237 mL) water
1 cinnamon stick
1 clove
1 star anise
2 pieces whole-blade mace
3 pieces whole juniper berries
Peel of 1 orange with no white pith
½ cup (65 g) goat cheese, room temperature

1. Peel the pears. Using a melon baller, carefully core the pears from the bottom.

2. Add the wine, honey, water, cinnamon stick, clove, star anise, mace, juniper berries, and orange peel to a saucepan large enough to also hold the pears submerged in liquid. Cover with a piece of parchment paper and heat to a low simmer. Occasionally, gently rotate the pears so they cook evenly. Poach 20 to 25 minutes, or until a small paring knife pierces the pears with little resistance. (The pears should hold their shape.)

3. Remove from the heat and let the pears stand in the poaching liquid until warm enough to handle. Remove the pears from the liquid, reserving 1 cup (237 mL) of the poaching liquid in the pan. Heat the reserved liquid to boiling and reduce until syrupy.

4. While liquid is reducing, spoon an equal amount of the goat cheese into each pear and plate. Glaze the pears with the reduced poaching liquid.

CONCORD GRAPE SAUCE

By **Paul Virant and Elissa Narow**, pastry chef, Perennial Virant

MAKES 1 CUP SAUCE (237 ML)

> **1 cup (80 g) Mick Klug Concord grapes**
> **2 tablespoons sugar**
> **1 tablespoon water**

1. Combine all the ingredients in a small saucepan. Heat to boiling over medium heat and cook 1 to 2 minutes. Puree, then strain through a sieve. Serve with assorted seedless Klug Farms grapes, cut into halves. Or, serve with Moscato Goat Cheesecake, page 180.

CHAPTER 7

SPENCE FARM

Marty, Kris, and Will Travis | Fairbury, Illinois | thespencefarm.com

When Marty, Kris, and Will get excited about something on their farm, which happens often, they start finishing each other's sentences. They are telling the story of how they started growing the rare Iroquois white corn on part of their 160 acres, and they are excited.

Kris: We got a grant from the Frontera Farmer Foundation for a white corn project.

Marty: Rick [Bayless]'s chef Brian Enyart came to us and said, "We used to get this corn from Iroquois Nation, and they're no longer doing it. Can you research it? If you can grow it, we need it." We found and bought a pound and a half of seed, which was $50 a pound …

Kris: …which is really a lot.

Marty: We planted it, and ended up with eight rows that looked like crap.

Will: And right when it was ready to pollinate, a windstorm came in and laid everything flat.

Kris: But we got enough where we got sixty-three pounds of cornmeal off of it, and we had …

Marty and Kris, together: … nine pounds of seed.

Kris: We took it to Brian and he was so happy, he was hugging the bag. And then he said, "Okay, next year, I need 8,000 pounds."

Their timing is perfectly in sync, a rhythm that has been perfected from working on the farm together, day after day. Marty, his wife, Kris, and his son, Will, are just as in tune with what they are growing. And they are growing a lot.

Will Travis carefully cultivates the Iroquois white corn.

Spence Farm was settled in 1830, and at the turn of the century, the farm comprised more than 1,000 acres dedicated to raising livestock. When the farm was passed down, it was split between families, and changed from being a livestock operation to a conventional farm of corn and soybeans.

Marty's grandmother farmed it industrially, but once Marty, Kris, and Will, showed up on the farm, they decided to return to traditional farming, without chemical inputs. In the last eight to 10 years, they removed all of the genetically modified crops on the farm. In the last few years, they removed the last of the corn and soybeans. "Most farmers would not survive on 160 acres today," says Marty. "But for us, the way we are farming, it's huge."

The Travises focus on growing specialty crops—like the rare white Iroquois corn, or a tomato from the Galapagos Island, or Jersey potatoes smuggled past customs by a friend in the U.K.—for chefs who have come to ask them for special and unusual requests.

"We're being really attentive to their needs, wants, and dreams, and helping to fulfill them," Marty says. "So if one says we'd really like to have local flour for pasta, we're going to figure out how to do it."

Two chefs in Chicago have asked Spence Farm to grow wheat for them: Stephanie Izard of Girl and the Goat, for her new West Loop diner focusing on daily fresh bread; and Jared Van Camp at Old Town Social, whose restaurant Nellcôte has its own flour mill to grind locally grown wheat for fresh pasta and pizza dough.

Two years ago, Marty started a new search for a specialty corn. Van Camp had asked him about a red corn, and Marty began to look. Eventually it got to the point where Marty sent out a mass email that said: "The first person who can find me 30 pounds of this corn gets 30 pounds of cornmeal free."

In the end, "Dad found it," Will says, with understated pride.

"I finally contacted the fellow who brought it into this country 10 years ago," Marty says, "and he sent us all of the seed that he had left in his private stock. It's in the ground now."

Just that morning, Marty had a request from a sous chef. He had green beans that his family brought from Slovenia that he wanted Spence Farm to help him preserve. It wasn't the first time that they have grown something with a personal family history.

"We've done that with beans that were here on this farm that the Kickapoo tribe had given to Marty's first great grandfather," Kris says. "A family member had grown them through the years."

Marty beams. "The same bean that was grown by the Native Americans 200 years ago, we are growing again. That's the treasure."

"It makes it exciting for us," Kris adds. "We're more interested in what restaurants are doing than the average delivery guy. It makes them start to think about what they could ask us to do, and it makes us start to think, what could we do? Every time we go to Chicago, we come back to the farm every week so inspired, instead of being tired, because on the way home we say. 'Oh, we need to get more seed for this, and find a space to plant this,' because we've talked to all of these people. It's really uplifting."

PLANTING SEEDS

The seeds in the ground aren't the only ones Marty and Kris are planting. Marty and Will moved back to his family farm in 1999, Kris joined in 2002. In 2003, they started working with chefs in Chicago. Shortly after, they began to get involved teaching the local community about their farming methods.

"We were invited by the Land Connection [an organization that educates farmers and the public about local food production] to go to a chef's collaborative meeting with six chefs," Marty says. "Rick Bayless was one of them. We were selling wild ramps, and they bought them. And they put us in touch with six other restaurants. It exploded from there, and it was all word of mouth."

From that connection, they learned about the Frontera Farmer Foundation grants. Will told his dad he wanted to resurrect the maple syrup business that used to be part of the farm.

"Native Americans showed my great, great, great, great grandfather how to make maple syrup," Marty says. "It was made and sold off of this farm as part of the farm enterprise, until the 1950s when my great grandfather died."

They wrote a grant and the Frontera Foundation paid for a portion of new equipment and a new syrup house that Will and a friend built.

As they grew their farm and created relationships with chefs in Chicago, the Travis family also started growing relationships between communities of farmers in Livingston County with their Stewards of the Land and Spence Farm Foundation.

Kris and Marty started Stewards of the Land in 2005 with three other farms as a way of organizing local farmers so that they could sell to local stores and chefs. Now they have limited membership to 25 farms, and there is a waiting list. Soon after, the couple started the Spence Farm Foundation, to "teach the art, history, and practice of small, sustainable family farming across America." The foundation holds regular

GET A TASTE OF SPENCE FARM

FRONTERA GRILL
fronterakitchens.com

THE BRISTOL
thebristolchicago.com

ACRE
acrerestaurant.com

IN FINE SPIRITS
infinespirits.com

GILT BAR
giltbarchicago.com

Will milks Surprise, the farm's Dexter cow, to prepare a bottle for her newborn calf. Marty looks on over his crops.

classes, workshops, and seminars, with a focus on new and young farmers. It works to support farm groups similar to Stewards of the Land, which helps connect local farmers with buyers, at local markets and at restaurants in Chicago.

For the Stewards, Marty and Kris take care of the Chicago restaurant side. Every week, Marty sends out an email to Chicago chefs with what is available from all of the farmers. The chefs place orders with Marty, who tells the farmers what to bring to the farm on Tuesday. Then they deliver to Chicago on Wednesday. In the first year, the Stewards of the Land farmers sold $1,500 in total. Last year, the group was at $1.2 million in sales.

"A lot of groups are set up for marketing purposes," Kris says. "But that's not our focus."

Marty chimes in. "Marketing happens, sales happen. But our goal is to continue to teach kids how to build relationships, not only to their communities, but also to each other and to chefs."

"It needs to go both ways," Kris says. "In order for chefs to have the best possible stuff, we have to help each other, because otherwise they're just another restaurant and you're just another farmer."

FROM THE FARMERS: Marty, Kris, and Will Travis

RESOURCES AND INSPIRATION

Frontera Farmer Foundation (rickbayless.com/foundation) has dramatically helped many small farms across the Midwest to expand and enter into markets in a more profitable way.

Two other resources that we find inspiring are **Small Farmer's Journal** (www.smallfarmersjournal.com), and **Acres USA** (www.acresusa.com). Both are publications that educate, inspire, and connect other small sustainable farmers across the country.

The Travis family loves growing unusual products for chefs, like these crunchy and concentrated radish pods that come from lettting radish plants go to seed.

STRADETTE WITH LITTLENECK CLAMS, GARLIC, AND CHILI PEPPERS

By **Jared Van Camp**, Old Town Social and Nellcôte

4 SERVINGS

"We grind the whole Red Floriani corn into corn flour to make a pasta noodle called 'Stradette' (Little Streets). Stradette is native to the Piedmont region of Italy and is actually an older version of the classic and more widely known 'Tajarin.' It predates Tajarin because corn flour was cheaper than wheat flour for centuries. Stradette pairs well with any shellfish, but we love making it with clams, garlic, and chili peppers. It makes for a great twist on the more common, Linguini & Clams."—Jared Van Camp

Stradette Pasta Dough (recipe follows)
6 quarts (5.69 L) water
Kosher salt
4–5 pounds (1.82 to 2.27 kg) littleneck clams, cleaned
2 cups (474 mL) white wine
¼ cup (59 mL) extra-virgin olive oil
8 cloves of garlic, peeled, thinly sliced
4 red jalapeño chili peppers, or other small red chilies, seeded, thinly sliced
¼ cup (12 g) thinly sliced basil leaves
4 tablespoons (57 g) unsalted butter

1. Prepare the Stradette Pasta Dough and refrigerate for at least 1 hour.

2. Roll out the pasta dough using the second thinnest setting of a pasta machine and cut into fettuccine-size noodles by hand or with the pasta cutting attachment of a stand mixer or pasta machine. Set aside.

3. Meanwhile, fill a large pot with 6 quarts of water and ⅓ cup (100 g) of kosher salt. Heat to boiling.

4. Cook the clams in the white wine in a covered pot on high heat until they open, about 4 minutes. Remove the clams and reserve. Strain the cooking liquid and reserve.

5. Heat the oil over low heat in a skillet and slowly toast the garlic slices to a golden brown. Immediately add the jalapeño pepper. (They should sizzle.) Stir the peppers and add the reserved white wine-clam liquid.

6. Drop the pasta into the boiling water and cook 2 minutes.

7. While the pasta is cooking, add the reserved clams and basil to the skillet. When the pasta is cooked, drain it and add it to the skillet with the butter. Toss mixture until well blended. Season to taste with salt. Serve immediately.

STRADETTE PASTA DOUGH

5 ounces (142 g) fresh milled corn flour
5 ounces (142 g) '00' semolina flour
2 eggs
½ ounce (15 mL) water

1. Mix the corn and semolina flours into a mound on a dry cutting board. Make a 'well' in the center of the mound and add the eggs and water. Slowly stir the eggs with a fork bringing a little bit of the flour mixture into the liquid ingredients with each circular stroke. When the dough seems to be coming together, start using your hands to fold the dough onto itself. Continue kneading the dough in this way for at least 5 minutes to develop the gluten. Wrap the dough in plastic wrap and refrigerate for at least 1 hour.

APPLE AND CELERY ROOT SALAD

By **Chris Pandel**, The Bristol and Balena

4–6 SERVINGS

- 1 Granny Smith apple, shaved
- ½ cup (78 g) celery root
- Salt
- ¼ bulb fennel
- 1 ounce (28 g) manchego cheese, marinated with 1 teaspoon heated elderflower liquor
- ¼ bunch watercress
- 1 tablespoon chopped topped hazelnuts

Marty, Will, and Kris Travis plan their day of chores in the morning light.

1 tablespoon chopped pickled chanterelle mushrooms
1 tablespoon chopped parsley
2 ounces (57 g) Apple Cider Vinaigrette (recipe follows)
Crushed toasted hazelnuts, for garnish

1. Dice the apple. Slice the celery root into paper-thin ribbons, and season gently with salt. Cut the fennel paper-thin slices. Toss the apple, celery root, fennel, cheese, watercress, chopped hazelnuts, and mushrooms in the vinaigrette just to coat. Arrange in a serving bowl and garnish with crushed hazelnuts.

APPLE CIDER VINAIGRETTE
2 cups (474 mL) apple cider
1 cup (237 mL) apple cider vinegar
1 teaspoon Dijon mustard
Zest and juice of 1 lemon
1 tablespoon (15 mL) elderflower liquor
1 tablespoon elderflower honey
1 cup (237 mL) grapeseed oil
½ cup (119 mL) olive oil
¼ cup (36 g) crushed toasted hazelnuts
2 shallots, minced
Salt and pepper to taste

1. Heat the apple cider to boiling in a small saucepan and reduce to about 1½ cups (356 mL). Cool. Combine the apple cider reduction, apple cider vinegar, mustard, lemon juice, elderflower liquor, and honey in a blender and blend. With the blender running, drizzle in the grapeseed and olive oils to emulsify. Remove from the blender and add the lemon zest, hazelnuts, and shallots. Season to taste with salt and pepper and cool.

GRILLED SHRIMP AND WHEAT BERRY SALAD

By **Carlos Ysaguirre**, Acre and Anteprima

4–6 SERVINGS

"This recipe consists of simple, humble ingredients. In order for the recipe to be great, we use ingredients of immaculate quality. Marty Travis provides such ingredients. This recipe highlights his passion, integrity, and knowledge of growing and harvesting great products."—Carlos Ysaguirre

1 cup (174 g) wheat berries
1 small onion, diced
1 small carrot, diced
2 stalks celery, diced
3 sprigs thyme
1 bay leaf
Salt
3 cups (711 mL) water
2 bunches of radishes (assorted varieties), thinly sliced
2 green tomatoes, cut into a medium dice
1 bunch parsley, chopped
2 lemons
8 tablespoons (119 mL) extra-virgin olive oil, divided
Pepper, to taste
20 peeled and deveined shrimp
Additional lemon juice

1. Put wheat berries, onion, carrot, celery, thyme, bay leaf, and a pinch of salt into a saucepan with the water. Heat to slow a simmer. Cook uncovered until the wheat berries are tender, about 45 minutes. Cool in liquid, then drain and transfer to a bowl.

2. Add the radishes, tomatoes, parsley, the zest and juice of 1 of the lemons, and 5 tablespoons (75 mL) of the oil. Season to taste with salt, pepper, and additional lemon juice.

3. Prepare a grill for direct cooking. Brush the shrimp with the remaining 3 tablespoons (45 mL) oil and season with salt and pepper. Grill the shrimp over medium heat 3 to 4 minutes on each side, or until cooked through. Serve the shrimp over the wheat berry salad.

When an 1860s school house was going to be burned or bulldozed a mile and a half down the road, Kris and Marty bought it for Spence Foundation and started hosting meetings and forums.

PART

2

MOVING FROM THE CITY TO THE FARM

It's easy to idealize a simple life on the farm: planting and growing, harvesting and eating. It may have been what initially attracted some of the farmers in the following pages. But these aren't just the dreamers; they are the doers. These are the farmers who left their urban lives, either partially or completely, to start from scratch or to take over a flailing farm. Most of them are first-time farmers who have specific, thoughtful ideas of how they want to grow food and raise animals. A few of these farms are three or four years old, while others—trailblazing farmers like David Cleverdon at Kinnikinnick, who started his work early on in the back-to-the-land movement—are nearing 20 years or more.

CHAPTER 8

BARE KNUCKLE FARM

Jess Piskor and Abra Berens | Northport, Michigan | bareknucklefarm.com

The story of how Abra Berens and Jess Piskor came together to farm a small plot of land nestled between fruit orchards far, far north on the lower peninsula of Michigan begins differently than most urban dwellers who set out to farm in the country. Before starting a farm from scratch, Abra and Jess barely knew each other.

Abra and Jess, along with Erik Hall (now Abra's husband), worked at Zingerman's Deli in Ann Arbor, Michigan. Erik connected Jess and Abra when he realized their two ambitions fit together perfectly. Abra had left Zingerman's to attend Ballymaloe Cookery School in southern Ireland, situated in the middle of an organic farm. When she returned, she realized she wanted to start a restaurant featuring a farm. Around the same time, Jess had been working on a farm in Ann Arbor a few days a week and realized he wanted to be a farmer, with a food business. When Abra moved to the farm in 2008, she and Jess knew of each other, but they didn't know each other very well. Nor did they know farming very well.

Luckily, their equally infectious smiles and contagious good natures fit well together, and they established Bare Knuckle Farm.

"We just sort of went for it," Jess says. "That first year, we were pretty small. We're still pretty small."

In just a few years, they've gained recognition from visiting Chicago chefs hosting dinners on the farm, and from Northport neighbor and celebrity chef Mario Batali, who listed them as a Leelanau County favorite in *Bon Appétit* magazine.

If there is a duo to represent the new face of small-scale farming, Jess and Abra are it. Even their cool logo is likely to catch the attention of other young farmers-to-be and local food followers. It's high on graphic design impact—a boxer holding a

carrot—and the name, which indicates their location on the Michigan "hand,"
is "honest, old-timey, and suggests hard work," Jess says.

THE LAND

Jess and Abra farm two acres where they grow 20 varieties of tomatoes, a
handful of carrots, including stubby orange Parisiennes, and long, nutrient-
dense Sugarsnax, curly kale, Red Russian kale, kohlrabi, Swiss chard, broccoli,
spring rutabaga, and collard greens all grow together in a small patch of land,
along with potatoes in heritage varieties like Adirondack Blue.

"We want to try to grow as much diversity as we can," Jess says. "We pride
ourselves on that, and on trying to get it all into people's mouths."

The place where they reach most of those people is at their market stall at
the Northport, Suttons Bay, and Traverse City farmers' markets throughout the

Opposite page: Abra restocks radishes at their Northport Farmer's Market booth. This page: Bare Knuckle Farm bags are for sale at the market, as is pour-over coffee by the cup.

summer. Abra suggests recipes to her market clients with nearly every product they sell, and shoppers listen attentively as she explains why she loves a particular vegetable, and how best to cook with it.

Meanwhile, behind her, Jess brews coffee by the cup—locally sourced beans from nearby Higher Grounds Coffee in Traverse City, that they roast on the farm themselves—on a double gas burner set up by their booth. The booth itself is a work of art, sturdy and beautiful boxes made out of half a dozen different woods and handcrafted by Jess during the slower winter months.

FARMING PRACTICES

As first-time farmers learning the ins and outs of doing everything themselves, they try something new on the farm every year. Two years ago, they started raising pigs. They had 18 the first year, and last year they bought 24. Most of the pigs spend time roaming and foraging underneath the organic cherry and apple trees of their neighbor's orchard—"they run under his trees and eat all of the bugs and rotten food that drops on the ground, clean up his orchard for him, and get fat along the way"—and six pigs are kept on their property because of their industriousness.

"They root up the soil and at the same time they are fertilizing it; they eat all of the weeds, all of the bugs," Jess explains. "In one of the areas last year, they made it more weed-free and fertile in 14 days than we could have all season." At the end of the season, they split a pig as their bonus, and sell the rest to chefs in Chicago.

Rob Levitt was one of the first takers of their pastured pig, to sell at his shop, The Butcher & Larder. "Rob was the first person who hired me in Chicago," Abra says, "and he's been really supportive. From the beginning he said if we could get the farm USDA-certified, then he would sell what we raise."

But the biggest change from bringing pigs to Bare Knuckle has come in the improvement in weeds and soil. "We are probably a weedier farm than most, because we're so young," Jess says. "When you first till up the ground, there are all of these seeds that are waiting underground, but after 10 years, if you stop the weeds from flowering, you start depleting their reserve of seeds. We are so much more weed-free because the pigs find all of those seeds."

Any weed control done at Bare Knuckle is done by hand—or by pigs—rather than chemicals, though Jess says they aren't striving to be certified organic. Because

their community of market clients and Chicago chefs is relatively small, Jess and Abra can explain to people directly how they grow their food, without the third party designation of organic.

"We like to say we are organic-ish," Jess says, smiling. "We don't want to use anything that is dangerous. We are aspiring to grow produce that you can put in your mouth without having to wash it. Also for us, we want to sell directly to people we know."

WORKING WITH CHEFS

A lot of the relationships they have are with chefs they do know, relationships Abra has built from living in Chicago in the winter and cooking for them.

"Paul Virant has been a great supporter—Abra worked for him at Vie for a number of years, so he has been really central," says Jess. "Nightwood has been really great to us as well." Abra worked at Vie for four years in the back and front of the house, and she also spent time cooking at Nightwood with Jason Vincent and at Floriole with Sandra Holl.

"The local food scene is really small, and it's not cut-throat," Abra says. "I remember when Chris Curren at Blue 13 wanted to bring in more local foods, he called Paul [Virant] who gave him a list of numbers and people to contact. It's such a supportive community in that sense."

Community is essential to Jess and Abra, who see it as a foundation for their growing business. They host monthly farm dinners at their cottage for friends and customers, which allows Abra to do some of the cooking she had hoped to be doing on the farm.

"It's been amazing to see how much Jess has grown as a farmer," Abra says. "It's our farm, but it's really starting to be on his schedule, which is great. Because I have neither the passion for it nor the skin tone," Abra laughs, referring to her fair, freckled skin. Their hope for the future is that Abra will take over a restaurant or prepared food business that is fed by the farm. For the time being, she is weeding and harvesting alongside Jess.

"Our idea of having the restaurant is that if Jess goes to market and comes back with something, then that goes into the kitchen," Abra says. "So it ab-

sorbs a lot of potential waste, and it's beneficial to the restaurant as well."

They have a lot of plans other plans, too. They want to put in a root cellar, add more permanent fencing, and start rotationally grazing their animals. With the Bare Knuckle business as a whole, they plan to add a restaurant, but also envision the possibility of expanding to include like-minded businesses—a B&B, or a local brewery or bakery—run perhaps by friends who want to relocate to the country.

"At this point, the sky seems to be the limit." Abra says with a smile.

FROM THE FARMERS: Jess Piskor | Abra Berens

RESOURCES AND INSPIRATION

Books

Nigel Slater's *Tender: A Cook and His Vegetable Patch* is a great book by an English cookery writer that has good recipes and gardening tips as well as different varieties and sources.

Hugh Fearnley-Whittingstall's *River Cottage* **Series**. The original book, the *River Cottage Meat Book* and the *River Cottage Preserves Handbook* are dog-eared and stained in my kitchen.

Chez Panisse Vegetables **and** *Chez Panisse Fruit*, **by Alice Waters**, are useful tools for shopping at the market and then finding a recipe to cook the goods just bought.

Organizations

The Land Connection (thelandconnection.org) run by Terra Brockman does lots of good work connecting young farmers to land and low-capital ways to start farming.

The Michigan Land Use Institute (mlui.org) helps facilitate sustainable use of Michigan's land and natural resources.

Agriculture

Eliot Coleman (fourseasonsfarm.com) has several gardening books and works with Johnny's Seeds (johnnyseeds.com) in Maine to provide information and high quality seeds for every sized garden.

Seed Saver's Exchange (seedsavers.org) out of Iowa has a wonderful collection of heirloom seeds that have been passed down through the generations of their seed-saving co-op.

RECIPE

ROASTED DELICATA SQUASH WITH WALNUTS AND RED ONION

"Delicata squash is my favorite squash when I'm in a pinch for time with dinner. The skins are tender and thin enough that you don't have to peel them. The richness of the squash pairs well with the tannins in the walnuts and the sharpness of the red onions."—Abra Berens

> 1 delicata squash, seeded
> Vegetable oil
> Salt and pepper
> ½ cup (50 g) walnuts, toasted
> 1 small red onion, sliced thinly
> 1 bunch parsley, leaves removed from the stems
> 2 tablespoons red wine vinegar

1. Cut the squash into ¼-inch (6-mm) half-moon slices. Heat a glug of the oil in a large skillet until it shimmers. Add the squash and season with salt and pepper. Cook the squash slices until brown on one side, then turn and cook until brown on the other side and the squash is tender.

2. While the squash is cooking, place the walnuts into a large resealable bag and hit with the bottom of a skillet or rolling pin until lightly broken. Combine the walnuts, onion, and parsley leaves in a large bowl. Add the squash to the onion and walnuts, and splash with the vinegar. Season to taste with salt and pepper, adding a good glug of olive oil if it doesn't taste rich and warming.

MIZUNA WITH RICOTTA AND BEETS, HAZELNUTS, PICKLED FENNEL, AND WARM SHERRY VINAIGRETTE

By **Duncan Biddulph**, Rootstock

4 SERVINGS

> **5 baby beets, scrubbed**
> **Salt**
> **6 ounces (170 g) ricotta, room temperature**
> **2½ ounces (75 mL) olive oil**
> **Pepper**
> **4 cups (240 g) mizuna, washed**
> **4 ounces (114 g) hazelnuts, toasted, chopped**
> **¾ cup (178 mL) Pickled Fennel (recipe follows)**
> **1 ounce (30 mL) sherry vinegar**

1. Place the beets in a saucepan and cover with cold water. Add fair measure of salt. Heat to boiling, then reduce heat, and simmer until the beets are tender, 10 to 15 minutes.

2. While the beets are cooking, whip the ricotta in a bowl with an electric mixer or with a wooden spoon, adding a few drops of the oil to improve the texture. Season to taste with salt.

3. Drain the beets, discarding the water, and quarter the beets while they are still warm. Return the beets to the pan and season liberally with salt and pepper. Whisk together the remaining oil and the vinegar and pour over the beets.

4. Combine the mizuna, half of the nuts, the pickled fennel, and the warm dressed beets, tossing quickly to prevent excessive wilting of the mizuna. Transfer the salad, a handful at a time, to a serving dish and add small spoonfuls of the whipped ricotta on and around the salad. Sprinkle with the remaining toasted hazelnuts, and a few cracks of black pepper.

PICKLED FENNEL

10 ounces (300 mL) water
6 ounces (180 mL) sherry vinegar
Fennel fronds, chopped
1 tablespoon sugar
2 teaspoons salt
1 teaspoon red chile flakes
2–3 fennel bulbs

1. Heat all the ingredients, except the fennel bulbs, to boiling. Meanwhile, peel the outer layer from the fennel bulbs. Cut the bulbs lengthwise in half, then slice the halves into thin lengthwise slices. Pour the vinegar mixture over the fennel. Cool and refrigerate.

SIX-HOUR ONION, DUROC SPOT BACON-CHERRY PUREE, FRIED TUSCAN KALE, AND KOHLRABI AND FENNEL SALAD

By **Nathan Sears and Paul Virant**, Vie

4–6 SERVINGS

> **4 onions (about 3 inches in diameter)**
> **Olive oil**
> **Salt and pepper**
> **8 ounces (227 g) fresh sour cherries, pitted**
> **2 ounces (57 g) Duroc Spot bacon, diced small**
> **2 ounces (57 g) sherry**
> **2 tablespoons (57 g) sherry vinegar**
> **2 stems thyme**
> **½ cup (114 g) water**
> **1 head kohlrabi**
> **1 fennel bulb**
> **8 ounces (227 g) Tuscan kale, washed, stemmed, thoroughly dried**

1. To prepare the onions, toss the onions with olive oil, and season with salt and pepper. Wrap in foil, place on a baking pan, and roast at 325°F (160°C) 4 hours. Remove the onions from the foil and continue roasting for 2 more hours, rotating every 30 minutes, or until the onions are soft throughout and evenly browned. If the center layers pop out of the onions, gently push them back. Remove from the oven and let cool. Then, using a serrated knife, carefully cut the onions crosswise into halves.

2. To prepare the bacon-cherry puree, cook the bacon in a small saucepan over low heat. When all the fat has been rendered from the bacon and the bacon begins to crisp, remove the bacon then add the cherries. Cook the mixture 3 or 4 minutes, then add the sherry, sherry vinegar, and thyme. Reduce the liquid until it is nearly gone, then add the water. Heat to boiling, cover, and cook 10 minutes. Transfer to a blender and blend until smooth, adding additional water, if needed. Season to taste with salt and pepper.

3. To prepare the kohlrabi and fennel salad, peel the outer part of the kohlrabi. Shave the kohlrabi into ¼-inch (6-mm) slices on a mandolin, or cut them into very thin slices. Stack the slices and julienne them. Trim the fennel's outer few leaves. Cut off the top fronds, reserving a few. Cut the fennel in half and remove the core. Shave the fennel into very thin slices on a mandolin. Toss the fennel, kohlrabi, bacon and reserved fronds in a bowl. (You will need ½ cup [119 mL] of vegetables per serving. Reserve the remaining kohlrabi and fennel for another use.) Toss the salad with olive oil and season to taste with salt and pepper.

4. To prepare the Tuscan kale, fill a large saucepan half full with olive oil and heat to 325°F (160°C). Carefully drop the kale into the oil. It will splatter. Fry about 1 minute, remove, and season to taste.

5. To serve, spoon about 2 tablespoons (30 mL) of the bacon-cherry puree onto each plate in a large circle. Place the bottom of each onion off to one side and the top leaning on the bottom. Place the kohlrabi and fennel salad off to the other side, and top with a few pieces of fried kale.

CHAPTER **9**

DIETZLER FARMS

Michelle Dietzler | Elkhorn, Wisconsin | dietzlerbeef.com

Cleetus Friedman, owner of City Provisions, a local food-focused market and deli in Ravenswood and a regular at the farmers' market, was one of the first chefs in Chicago to start buying Dietzler Farms beef. This is the story he tells:

> After I came up with my business model, I didn't have relationships with farmers. I knew them from going to markets, but I didn't have relationships because I had no reason to. In 2007, I was working at Heaven on Seven, doing regular monthly chef events. During a graduation party event, I was introduced to Michelle's product. The host came up to me with a couple of steaks and said, "Put these steaks on the grill and give them back to me." And I said, "What's so good about them?" And she tells me they came from her neighbor who has a local farm, that she's coming by later, and she'll introduce me to her. So I met Michelle Dietzler, who told me how her farm was just getting started. She gave me a ribeye and said, "This is a sample of what we're doing." The next night I put it on the grill, and it was the best steak I'd ever had. I said to my wife, "This is crazy good; this is going to be the beginning of my business."

Michelle Dietzler isn't exactly who you imagine when you think *cattle farmer*. She spends as much time in the city as she does on the farm, but there is no denying that when it comes to running her family's Dietzler Farms, she is as dedicated as the farmer whose nails are embedded with dirt. In a handful of years, she is responsible for turning her family's hobby farm in Wisconsin into what might be Chicago's most sought-after beef.

Michelle is a young journalist-turned-farmer who started out with a couple dozen cows raised in Elkhorn, Wisconsin. About six years ago, Michelle started selling at farmers' markets in Wisconsin. Then she started knocking on peoples' doors—chefs' doors. Naturally skilled at marketing and making connections, Michelle talked to every chef she could. "Everybody had my card, so once things really started to happen, they were able to call me," she says.

In their first year selling to chefs, the Dietzlers started with 35 animals; last year they sold more than 250.

CUSTOMIZED BEEF

Michelle says chefs were initially slow to catch on. The beef was expensive, and many chefs wanted to be able to place orders at the last minute.

"They just wanted to call the night before and say, 'Deliver tomorrow,'" Michelle says. "And they couldn't do that with me. I have to know ahead of time so I know how many animals to raise. And my whole thing is customization, so they had to take a step back and realize, 'If I want it custom-raised for me, I have to agree to buy it.' That was a really weird thing for them to grasp."

Michelle wanted to customize her beef for chefs, and she wanted to sell it fresh. A lot of people encouraged her to do frozen because it was easier, but Michelle and the chefs whom she was working with wanted it fresh.

Michelle speaks highly of chef Paul Virant, who she says helped shape her business from the beginning. "He said, 'Can you do it fresh? Can you dry age it 28 days? Can you do these cuts?' I said yes to everything, having no idea if I could, and then figured it out from there," she says.

Before Dietzler Farms started distributing to chefs, they only had their animals cut in basic ways: steaks, roasts, and hamburger. When they ran the numbers, the wholesale prices didn't make sense, and their business would have been limited to retail only.

Michelle started researching to learn about additional cuts, and learned about all the cuts that they had just been grinding into burger, from short ribs to beef cheek. She started testing recipes and discovered the range of cuts could expand the way they could sell beef. Delis wanted brisket, charcuteries were looking for liver and beef heart, and certain pastry chefs used the suet.

And some chefs, like Virant, bought the whole cow and found a use for almost everything.

"We learned how to process it and what to do with it all," Virant says. "As far as working with all of the different cuts and developing a plan for every-thing, that's a whole challenge, what to do with this and that. We did tasso-style beef sirloin, pastrami, corned beef, and sausages."

Now every week, five to seven cattle are taken down to the processor where they are slaughtered, then hung for 21 days of dry aging. Then, they're custom cut for chefs.

"Our butcher is awesome," Michelle says. "He will call the chefs, and say, "'Hey chef, I'm cutting this for you, how exactly do you want me to do this?' It's really cool."

GOOD MEAT

"We raise cattle from birth to harvest, and we raise all of our own feed," Michelle says. "And we start with the best genetics."

The farm raises three different breeds: Black Angus, Hereford, and Red Angus. Michelle says Hereford are the easiest to work with, but Angus are known for being high yielding, well-marbled animals.

"We do DNA and ultrasound tests for the tenderness gene, so when we pick bulls, we know their ribeye area, their carcass data—that is very impor-

Opposite page: Michelle's brother Bob gets ready to move the pasturing cows.
Right: Dietzler Farms on an idyllic blue-sky day.

tant to us because ultimately we are selling meat, not just a heavy animal," explains Michelle.

All of the calves drink their mother's milk and then get turned out onto pasture to graze in rotation, which means the cows eat the grass down in one section of pasture before they are moved in order for the grass to grow back. Once there is no more grass, they are fed hay, non-genetically modified alfalfa grown on Dietzler land.

Once the cattle reach about 600 pounds, which can take anywhere from four to six months depending on the season, they are moved to an area where they are just on grass, usually out on pasture. For the final 90 days, they are brought into a smaller sized sorting pen where they are finished with what Michelle calls their signature Wisconsin diet, including corn grown on the farm.

Although the Dietzlers could raise 100-percent grass-fed animals, and it would be more cost effective, they see the flavor they create as distinctive of their beef.

"It's more of an art, I think, than just a commodity operation," says Michelle. "We are doing something that everyone won't be able to do. That makes us specialty, boutique beef. For us it's about a really tender piece of meat, that has a lot of flavor, and that is a throwback to what people used to eat in this area. We have this land in Colorado, and yeah, it would be way cheaper to feed them out there on grass, but you are going to get a completely different flavor than our Wisconsin beef here. We want to be different from everyone else, we don't want to buy someone else's formula."

CHANGING SEASONS

By the summer of 2011, Dietzler beef was being sold to dozens of restaurants in Chicago, with a growing wait list. The Dietzlers found themselves faced with a decision: do they try to continue to increase production? Or do they continue to raise their animals as they always had, on the same scale? Faced with the pressures of expediting the production of the animals to meet more demand, they decided to stay true to their practices and realize they wouldn't be able to keep up with demand. Instead of continuing to distribute year-round and pushing to meet a growing production schedule, Dietzler beef is now only available during the summer and fall.

According to Michelle, "It is the most sustainable way to continue producing the beef that chefs have come to appreciate."

So just like the anticipation that comes from waiting for asparagus or tomato season, chefs look forward to the time of year when Dietzler beef is in season.

Michelle's dad worked on this vintage Massey-Harris tractor so that it now functions on the farm.

FROM THE FARMER: Michelle Dietzler

RESOURCES AND INSPIRATION

The Meat Buyer's Guide was to create a bridge between the farm that had always sold in live weight and the chefs that had been buying commodity from meatpacking houses.

While we don't agree with every last detail in ***The Omnivore's Dilemma***, by Michael Pollan, our farm believes in the same message.

RECIPE

BBQ BEEF SANDWICHES

"Burgers are always a great way to feed our huge family in the summer, but sometimes it's hard to find a volunteer to cook at the hot grill in the afternoon sun. We started using our Dutch oven or slow cooker to make BBQ Beef sandwiches. A chuck roast, arm roast, brisket, or even a sirloin tip roast works well for this."—Michelle Dietzler

1 (3½-pound [1.59-kg]) beef roast, such as a chuck or arm roast

1 bottle of your favorite barbecue sauce (or make your own)

Slow Cooker Preparation: Brown the beef roast on all sides in oil in a large skillet. Place the beef in the slow cooker and pour the barbecue sauce over top. Cook on low heat 8 hours. Remove the beef from the slow cooker, and using 2 large forks, shred the beef. Return the beef to the slow cooker set on the *warm* setting. Serve with buns for sandwiches. To serve these sandwiches for lunch, start cooking the beef before you go to bed and shred it the next morning. Lunch is ready whenever you are!

Dutch Oven Preparation: Brown the beef roast on all sides in oil in the Dutch oven over medium-high heat. Pour the barbecue sauce over top. Roast at 350°F (180°C) until beef is tender, 4 to 5 hours. Remove the beef from the oven, and using 2 large forks, shred the beef. Return beef to the Dutch oven and serve on buns.

GRILLED DIETZLER FARMS CHIMICHURRI-RUBBED SKIRT STEAKS

By **Randy Zweiban**, Province

4 SERVINGS

> 1 cup (24 g) Thai basil leaves
> ½ cup (8 g) cilantro leaves
> ½ cup (24 g) snipped chives
> ½ tablespoon chopped red onion
> ½ cup (119 mL) olive oil
> ½ teaspoon sherry vinegar
> ½ teaspoon kosher salt
> 2 tablespoons chopped jalapeño pepper
> ½ teaspoon honey
> ½ tablespoon freshly toasted and ground cumin
> 1 tablespoon roasted garlic puree
> 4 (8-ounce [227-g]) Dietzler Farms skirt steaks

1. To prepare the chimichurri, blanch the basil, cilantro, and chives in boiling water 10 seconds, then shock in ice water. Place herbs and all the remaining ingredients, except the steaks into a blender and pulse until roughly smooth.

2. Marinate the steaks in some of the chimichurri for a few hours or overnight. Prepare a grill for direct cooking. Grill the steaks to medium-rare, basting with more chimichurri. Let the steaks rest before slicing. Cut each of the steaks into 4 or 5 slices, fan out the slices on plates, and serve with the chimichurri.

BEER-BRAISED SHORT RIBS

OVER SWEET POTATO MASH, WITH APPLE CIDER SYRUP AND ONION FRIZZLES

By **Cleetus Friedman**, City Provisions

4–6 SERVINGS

10 pounds (4.54 kg) beef short ribs (brisket or flat iron can be substituted)

4 bottles Scotch ale or any medium-bodied amber ale

2 bunches flat-leaf parsley

1 head garlic, cloves peeled and finely chopped

3 teaspoons pepper

1 bay leaf

2 tablespoons kosher salt

About 1 cup (237 mL) olive oil

3 cups (450 g) diced onions

2½ cups (300 g) diced celery

2 cups (256 g) diced carrots

6 cups (1.42 L) chicken broth

Sweet Potato Mash (recipe follows)

Cider Syrup (recipe follows)

Onion Frizzles (recipe follows)

1. Place short ribs in a large bowl. Add ale, parsley, garlic, bay leaf, and pepper. Let marinate in the refrigerator for 12 to 24 hours. (The longer it marinates, the more flavorful the braised ribs will be.)

2. Remove the ribs from the marinade and reserve the marinade. Pat ribs dry and season with salt and additional pepper. Heat ¼ cup (59 mL) of the oil in a 12-inch (30-cm) skillet over medium-high heat just until smoking. Working in 3 batches, sear the ribs until brown on both sides, wiping the skillet clean and adding ½ cup (119 mL) of oil before the second and third batches.

3. Transfer the ribs to a 3- to 4-inch-deep (7.5- to 10-cm) roasting pan, placing the ribs, bone sides up, in a single layer. Without cleaning the skillet, add the onions, celery, and carrots to the skillet. Sauté over medium heat until the onions are translucent.

4. Transfer vegetables to large saucepan, being sure to scrape up any brown bits from bottom and side of the skillet. Add reserved marinade and heat to boiling. Simmer until pan is almost dry, about 1 hour. Add chicken broth and heat to boiling. Pour the broth mixture over the ribs and cover the roasting pan with foil.

5. Braise at 325°F (160°C) until the short ribs are tender and falling off the bones, about 2 hours. Remove from the oven and cool about 10 minutes. Remove and discard any excess fat and bones. Transfer the meat to bowl, cover with foil, and keep warm.

6. Prepare the Sweet Potato Mash.

7. Prepare the Cider Syrup.

8. Prepare the Onion Frizzles.

9. To serve, spoon sweet potato mash on to serving plates and top with the short ribs. Garnish with onion frizzles and drizzle with the cider syrup.

SWEET POTATO MASH

6 pounds (2.72 kg) sweet potatoes
1 stick (½ cup [114 g]) unsalted butter, melted
½ cup (119 mL) heavy cream, warmed
1 teaspoon salt
½ teaspoon pepper

1. Using a fork, prick each sweet potato twice and place in a foil-lined shallow baking pan. Roast the potatoes in the lower third of the oven at 400°F (200°C) until they are very tender, about 1 hour. Remove and cool slightly. Halve the potatoes lengthwise and scoop out the warm flesh into a large bowl. Mash the potatoes with a potato masher. Stir in the butter, cream, salt, and pepper.

(Continued on next page)

ONION FRIZZLES

2 very large onions, cut crosswise into thin slices
About 3½ cups (424 g) all-purpose flour
Salt
1 egg
1 cup (237 mL) buttermilk
About 2 cups (300 g) plain fine dry breadcrumbs
About 1 quart (948 mL) vegetable oil

1. Separate onion slices into rings.

2. Stir together flour and a pinch of salt in a bowl. Whisk together egg and milk in another bowl. Spread breadcrumbs out on a plate. Dredge onions in the flour mixture, shaking off excess, then dip in egg mixture, letting excess drip off, and coat with breadcrumbs. Transfer to sheets of wax paper.

3. Heat oil in a large saucepan over medium-high heat. Fry onion rings in batches of 4 to 6, without crowding, turning over once or twice, until golden brown, about 3 minutes per batch. Transfer to paper towels to drain.

CIDER SYRUP

½ gallon (1.90 L) fresh apple cider

1. Pour the cider into a large pot. Heat to boiling. Simmer until the cider is reduced to a syrupy consistency, about 45 minutes.

DIETZLER FARMS THAI BEEF SIRLOIN CURRY

By **Paul Virant**, Perennial Virant and Vie

4–6 SERVINGS

> 1 pound (454 g) Dietzler Farm beef sirloin, cut into 1-inch (2.5-cm) cubes
>
> Salt and pepper
>
> 3 tablespoons (45 mL) canola oil
>
> 1 tablespoon butter
>
> 3 carrots, diced
>
> 1 large onion, diced
>
> 2 stalks celery, diced
>
> 2 cups (130 g) stemmed green curly kale leaves cut into 1-inch (2.5-cm) strips
>
> 6 cloves garlic, minced
>
> 1 jalapeño pepper, diced
>
> 3 tablespoons (18 g) Madras curry powder
>
> Zest and juice of 2 limes
>
> 2 teaspoons fish sauce
>
> 1 can (14 ounces [420 mL]) coconut milk
>
> Water
>
> 1 cup (24 g) basil leaves, cut into strips, for garnish
>
> Cooked jasmine or sticky rice

1. Season the beef with salt and pepper. Heat the oil in a large skillet over medium-high heat and sear the beef until brown on all sides. Remove from skillet and reserve.

2. Melt the butter in the same skillet and add the carrots, onion, celery, kale, garlic, and jalapeño pepper. Cover and sweat over low heat 5 minutes. Uncover and add the curry powder, lime zest, and fish sauce. Cook 1 minute, then add the coconut milk and 1 to 2 cups of water. Heat to boiling, add the beef, and cook until the sauce is the desired consistency. Season to taste with salt, and pepper. Finish with basil and lime juice. Serve with jasmine or sticky rice.

CHAPTER 10

KINNIKINNICK FARM

David Cleverdon | Caledonia, Illinois | kinnikinnickfarm.com

The day is starting at Kinnikinnick Farm, and David Cleverdon has a lot to do. His sheep are hungry, his goats needs milking, he needs to finish writing a task list for the farm interns, a couple hundred baby chicks are about to show up at the local post office for pickup, and he has a mother-daughter duo visiting the farm for a few nights, who are looking for something interesting to see. On top of everything, the Internet is down.

David is used to juggling a lot at once, and seems to add on more at every chance he gets. He has been certified organic since 1994, and has just begun to introduce livestock into his farm. He just ordered the equipment to start making butter and yogurt with the milk from his new Nubian milking goat, which he'll do sometime after he starts pressing apple cider and before he starts making sausages with the feeder pigs he hopes to add. He has a lot of plans.

David is on the board of Green City Market, and the board of Frontera Farmer Foundation. He knows a lot of people—"all the players"— in the local food community of Chicago, in part because he's been in it for so long, in part because he likes to talk. He tells good stories and has a lot to say—but you'll have to keep up, David talks fast and he doesn't have much time to waste.

"We aren't just a production farm," says David, of his 100-plus acres in Caledonia, Illinois. "We started doing this because we're interested in the food part of farming—everything about food: how it's grown, produced, used, celebrated; how it's a part of life itself; that it's how people connect with each other, with themselves. The sacrament of eating, I guess that is what we're addressing."

He stops abruptly. "Excuse me, I gotta go scrape chicken shit."

THIRD GIG

"This is my third gig," David says. "And if you told me that at this point in my life, I'd be scraping chicken shit …"

David first came to Chicago in 1963 to graduate school at the University of Chicago.

His first gig was politics, where he "got involved in every good-guy, good-cause losing political campaign you could imagine."

After a few winning campaigns, David ended up working as a staffer for the governor of Illinois. When his boss didn't win a second term, he was suddenly out of a job. He went to the Chicago Board of Trade, where he worked for 11 years. He raised a family, made a living, and somewhere along the way bought the farm property in Caledonia—170 acres, with a crumbling farmhouse. When his last child went to college, he and his wife, Susan, moved to the farm. They sold their house in Wisconsin, their co-op in Hyde Park, put all of their belongings in storage, bought a 30-foot trailer and moved to the farm. For three years, and three winters, they lived in the trailer on the farm, "within three inches of disaster," David says—meaning the thickness of the trailer walls—and figured out what to do next.

David and Susan had always had a big garden. It got bigger and bigger, until David says he realized he didn't need a garden, he needed a farm. Enter David's third gig: farming. In 1993, they started farming their land. David calls it their "zero year; nothing worked." In the next year, they learned from their mistakes, and got organic certification.

"I like to say that good judgment comes from experience, and experience comes from bad judgment," David says. "This whole place becomes a workshop in chaos theory. Because everything is related, it's all about solving the prior problem."

For David, the farm is endlessly fascinating. They are always pushing and trying to expand, like adding livestock to the farm.

David takes care of feeding the chickens and goats every morning; day-old chicks arrive to Kinnikinnick Farm via USPS.

ANIMALS

The baby chicks come in the mail, all 250 of them, chirping through holes in the cardboard box they are shipped in. David raises chickens for eggs (layers) and chicken for meat (broilers). Most of his broiler birds are Cornish Crosses, a common bird that grows quickly. Then he finishes the season with Kosher King, a slow-growing, black-feathered chicken with a great taste.

For the layers, the farm has 45 black-and-white Barred Rocks, 45 brown-and-grey Araucanas that lay beautiful blue eggs, and a few of a rare breed called Chantecler. David says they are adding 45 Marans, a breed that lays a chocolate brown colored egg.

David pastures his broiler birds to help to fertilize the soil. He recently brought a few sheep and goats to the farm, hoping to build them into his vegetable growing rotation, but soon realized that ruminant animals, like sheep, goats, and cows that graze and forage need larger pastures.

Now he wants to add feeder pigs, to help fertilize and root up the soil by digging weeds—an incessant problem on an organic farm that does weeding by hand. Once the feeder pigs have torn through a patch of land, fertilizing it and clearing it of weeds, he can follow with vegetables.

VEGETABLES

David grows a lot: asparagus, arugula, turnips, radishes, beets, cucumbers, tomatoes, lettuces, leeks, peas, and squashes—among many others—but he is especially known for his Italian cooking greens: Bietina, Cavolo Nero, Minestra Nera, and Spigariello, greens that most chefs in Chicago didn't have a source for before David grew them.

He also recently started growing Espelette peppers, a staple of Basque cuisine, only designated as such if grown in the town of Espelette in Southern France.

"I'm the only one growing these things," David says. "A guy I know got them from his source in England, and he gave them to me, a few others, and one seed company—so you're going to start seeing them around. Paul Kahan says it's the most complicated pepper, taste-wise."

Above: Coops are home to Barred Rock and Araucana chickens, and a Chantecler rooster. Below: Farm workers harvest arugula for market.

THE FARM

David has a required reading list for his interns and field hands who come to work at Kinnikinnick Farm: Wendell Berry's *The Unsettling of America: Culture and Agriculture*, and Albert Murray's *Stomping the Blues*.

"When Americans do things well, they play jazz," David says, explaining the second, non-agriculture book. "My goal is to farm the way that Murray's musicians play jazz."

Jazz is difficult to define, but if you think of it as a musical creation, a series of improvised countermelodies that carry you along in a sometimes seemingly unorganized path, yet always find their way back to the main melody, then David's farming seems like jazz.

Anyone visiting for a day, or perhaps staying at one of the Featherdown tents for a few nights, will quickly get a taste of Kinnikinnick Farm and the big personality of David Cleverdon.

Kinnikinnick is part of the agritourism movement that has spread across the ocean from Europe. The farm is home to several Featherdown tents, rustically chic structures imported from Holland, complete with charmingly mismatched chairs, an eclectic mix of pots, pans, and cooking tools. They also feature a wood burning stove to boil water for French press coffee, or cook fresh sausages and eggs, which are available from the farm's Honesty Shop. Guests can wander around, and get a feel for life on the farm.

The farm also hosts a few dinners throughout the season, events where chefs from Chicago visit and cook, including many chefs who have been long-time friends.

THE CHEFS

Though just a few years ago Kinnikinnick Farm sourced its vegetables to as many as 50 different chefs, David says they have boiled down to just working with the 15 or so who were always very consistent. He says he likes to work with the chefs who have their own restaurants or are a principal in the business, chefs who are passionate about what they do, the ones who are "focused and intense."

Bruce Sherman, Sarah Stegner, Carrie Nahabedian, Jason Hammel—just to name a few. As he starts listing them, he keeps adding to the list as he remembers more.

"Oh, and Jared, one of my favorite guys—I only want to do hogs because of Jared Van Camp. And Paul Kahan—I love Paul Kahan. He and his wife come about once a year just to hang out."

GREEN CITY MARKET

David began going to the Evanston farmers' market shortly after he began farming, and Kinnikinnick Farm is still there every Saturday. Not long after he started selling there, Abby Mandel began to recruit farmers for her ambitious Green City Market.

"She would show up at the Evanston farmers' market on Saturday and say, 'When am I going to see this stuff at my market?' At that time we were one of the few organic growers; our stand looked spectacular. And I let her know, 'Abby, you can push a lot of people around and terrify every chef in the world—but not me.' She finally got the message, and began to say things like, 'Please,'" David starts laughing. "And then I came to the market, and we quickly became very good friends."

David starting doing speaking engagements with Abby, who recruited him to join the steering committee for Green City Market, and then later the board.

"That's what's unusual about Abby Mandel," David says. "Most people who are like her don't do what she did—she began to institutionalize what she had done. She built a board. She built a whole planning process, and a strategic plan. Green City Market is great, and it's all because of her."

FROM THE FARMER: David Cleverdon

RESOURCES AND INSPIRATION

I revisit these authors frequently and recommend these books to anyone interested in working at Kinnikinnick or understanding what it is that we do here:

Wendell Berry's **The Unsettling of America** has been a pivotal book in my life. It is about life, work, and virtue. Susan and I had always talked about farming but after I read *Unsettling*, the talk stopped. I knew what I had to do. I've been doing it ever since.

Albert Murray's **Stomping the Blues** helped me make sense of the world. For me, it is more than a book about music. Albert Murray is the quintessential American. He describes the discipline Americans employ to do things well when they do things in a uniquely American way. My goal is to farm the way Murray's musicians play music.

Louis Bromfield's **Pleasant Valley** (1943), **Malabar Farm** (1947), and **From My Experience** (1955). Bromfield's political and cultural point of view and his agriculture were uniquely American. His farming methods became the road not taken by American agriculture this past half century. But its validity remains, attested to by the recent rise of grass-based farming. Bromfield is one of the reasons we have started to bring livestock on to Kinnikinnick Farm.

KINNIKINNICK FARM'S GREENS BALLS

Here is the basic preparation technique for cooking Kinnikinnick's Italian Greens, such as Bietina, Cavolo Nero, Minestra Nera, and Spigariello, or Swiss chard.—David Cleverdon

Use greens with a little tooth remaining in the leaf, not "cooked to death." This results in a glistening mound on the plate without a watery puddle. Set a large pot of salted water on to boil. Wash the greens well in a sink of cold water and drain in a colander. Remove the fibrous stems by grasping the stem in one hand and pulling the leaf away. Roughly slice the leaves into ½-inch (13-mm) ribbons. (This step is not essential unless the greens are going to be mixed right away with pasta or rice.) Blanch the greens very briefly in the boiling water and cool them quickly in a sink filled with ice water. (To make blanching easier, use a pasta pot with a lift-out strainer/steamer, because you can quickly process a large volume of greens in small batches, while keeping the water at or near the boil.) Drain the greens and form them into tennis ball-sized mounds between your hands or on a clean kitchen towel and squeeze out the excess moisture. Wrap and store the "balls" of greens for a day or two in the refrigerator until you are ready to use them. When you are ready, you can chop the "balls" of greens and use them in any number of ways.

Here are some of our favorites:

- Simply sautéed with butter or with garlic and olive oil
- In pasta, with garlic, sautéed onions, and pancetta
- Added to a skillet of sausages and pan-roasted potatoes
- Added to lentil soup 5 minutes before serving
- Mixed into a skillet of quick-cooking couscous, with currants and toasted pine nuts
- With chickpeas in a spicy tomato sauce

HALIBUT BACCALÀ, ROASTED BEETS, PISTACHIOS, AND ORANGES

By **Jared Van Camp**, Old Town Social and Nellcôte

4 SERVINGS

"Dave Cleverdon is someone I clicked with the first time I ever met him. He's a man that makes you smile. Kinnikinnick is a special place. So special, that I am in fact getting married at the farm in 2013. My fiancée and I spent one of our first dates camping out on the farm. Dave's beets are something to treasure. I have no idea what the scientific reason would be behind why his beets are so much sweeter, earthier, and just flat-out better tasting than anybody else's, but they are, hands down, the best beets I've ever tasted."—Jared Van Camp

Note: The baccalà in this recipe is time consuming, but incredibly fulfilling if you're up to the task! We feel like the halibut provides a much softer, almost buttery texture to the finished product than the more traditional (and overfished) Atlantic Cod.

> **Halibut Baccalà (recipe follows)**
> **Roasted Beets (recipe follows)**
> **3 oranges**
> **3 tablespoons (45 mL) champagne vinegar**
> **½ cup (76 g) pistachio nuts, toasted and roughly chopped**
> **¼ cup (8 g) loosely packed tarragon leaves**
> **Salt and pepper, to taste**

1. Prepare the Halibut Baccalà. This will take 2 weeks.

2. On the last day of the baccalà preparation, prepare the Roasted Beets.

3. Break the baccalà into natural pieces and arrange on a platter. Use a little of the residual oil to "dress" the fish on the platter.

4. Zest the oranges. Peel the oranges and section them by cutting along the membranes that separate the sections (supremes). Add the zest, orange supremes, vinegar, nuts, tarragon to the bowl of beets, adding about ½ cup (119 mL) of the leftover olive oil from the baccalà. Toss gently until well mixed. Season to taste with salt and pepper. Arrange on the platter on top of the baccalà. Serve.

HALIBUT BACCALÀ

1 pound (454 g) boneless, skinless fresh Alaskan Halibut (preferably center cut)

¾ ounce (21 g) kosher salt

2 quarts (1.90 L) whole milk, divided

3 stems fresh thyme

2 cloves garlic, crushed

5–6 whole black peppercorns

2 cups (474 mL) extra-virgin olive oil

1. Sprinkle the fish evenly with the salt. Wrap in plastic wrap, place in shallow glass dish, and refrigerate for 7 days.

2. Unwrap the fish and place back in the dish. Refrigerate, uncovered, 7 more days, making sure everyday to wipe up any liquid the fish releases.

3. When the fish is fully cured, place it in a small container with 1 quart (948 mL) of the milk. Cover and refrigerate overnight.

4. The next day, remove the halibut from the milk and place in a small saucepan with the remaining 1 quart (948 mL) of the milk, the thyme, garlic, and peppercorns. Slowly heat this mixture to simmering, and immediately turn off the heat and remove the fish from the liquid.

5. Cover the warm fish with the olive oil. (The fish may flake a little into pieces). Let the fish cool in the refrigerator.

ROASTED BEETS

3 cups (900 g) kosher salt

6 baby red beets, tops removed

6 baby yellow beets, tops removed

6 baby Chioggia beets, tops removed

1. Spread the salt onto the bottom of a shallow roasting pan. Place the beets on the salt and cover the pan with foil.

2. Roast the beets at 350°F (180°C) until tender, 50 to 60 minutes. Remove from the oven. When cool enough to handle, peel the beets, cut into halves or quarters and place them into a large glass bowl. Chill in the refrigerator.

KINNIKINNICK FARM ITALIAN BRAISING GREENS

By **Sarah Stegner and George Bumbaris**, Prairie Grass Cafe

4–6 SERVINGS

"Dave is famous among the chefs for his amazing Italian Braising Greens. They have intense flavor and color. He does a really great job of harvesting them just when they need to be picked. If the leaves are very young and it is early in the season you do not need to remove the stems."—Sarah Stegner

> **2 pounds (908 g) Italian braising greens**
> **1 small onion, peeled and diced**
> **1 tablespoon thinly sliced garlic chives**
> **Salt and pepper**
> **3 tablespoons (45 mL) olive oil**
> **2 tablespoons sweet butter**

1. Remove and discard the stems from the greens. Cook the leaves in a large pot of boiling salted water until tender but still bright green. Immediately, transfer the greens to a bowl of ice water. When the greens are cool, gently squeeze out any excess water. Reserve.

2. Sauté the onion in the olive oil in a large skillet over medium heat until tender. Add the garlic chives and sauté until tender. Season with the salt and pepper and add the butter. When the butter melts and bubbles, stir in the greens and cook until they are hot.

LITTLE GEM SALAD WITH BUTTERMILK DRESSING

By **Paul Kahan and Brian Huston**, The Publican

> 1 slice of bread
> 1 clove garlic, cut in half
> 4 heads Little Gem lettuce
> 1 fennel bulb, thinly sliced on a mandolin
> 3 radishes, thinly sliced on a mandolin
> 12 basil leaves, torn
> Buttermilk Dressing (recipe follows)

1. To prepare croutons, toast bread in a toaster or in 350°F (180°C) oven until golden brown and toasted through. Remove from the oven and immediately rub both sides of the toast with garlic. Cool and coarsely chop the toast into little pieces.

2. Meanwhile, prepare the buttermilk dressing.

3. Combine the lettuce, fennel, radishes, basil, and croutons. While tossing the salad, slowly pour in the dressing until the salad is heavily dressed.

BUTTERMILK DRESSING

> ½ cup (119 mL) buttermilk
> ¼ cup (59 mL) sherry vinegar
> 1 shallot, minced

1. Whisk all the ingredients together.

CHAPTER 11

LEANING SHED FARM

Dave and Denise Dyrek | Berrien Springs, Michigan | leaningshed.com

Before he started farming, Dave Dyrek and his wife, Denise, had a big garden with nearly 400 tomato plants. "Tomatoes are my favorite. I love to eat them, to look at them, the colors and the shape—everything about them," Dave says, gushing a little. But with 400 plants, he had more than he knew what to do with. For Dave, the turning point came the first time he showed his tomatoes to chefs.

A friend of his was a partner at a Chicago restaurant, and suggested he should take them to the chef there. Dave remembers arriving at the restaurant and walking into the kitchen through the backdoor. The dishwasher, the chef, and a couple of prep guys were at work. Dave carried in his boxes of tomatoes and as soon as he popped the lids off, the crew stopped what they were doing to crowd in and admire the bounty of heirloom tomatoes. "They were truly beautiful," Dave admits, "and for me there was a change. I was like, 'Oh, yeah, I'm going to do this.'"

Until then, Dave and his wife Denise were living in Chicago and spending time on a small 30-acre farm they had bought in 2004, in Berrien Springs, Michigan, for weekend getaways. Their garden grew every year, until it had gotten where they were spending more time working in their garden than they were cruising around the area like they used to. And they grew more than they could eat themselves or give away to friends. It didn't take long, after Dave saw the reaction of that first Chicago chef, for him to sell his heating and air conditioning business and move to the farm fulltime.

"Part of it is like my mid-life crisis," Dave laughs. "At times I love it, I do, I really love it, and at times, it's like—what the heck did I do? I always worked hard, but never like this—seven days a week, morning to night!"

GROWING ORGANICALLY

Leaning Shed isn't certified organic, but Dave and Denise have been farming organically since they started. "At first, we were gardening," says Dave, "and it was stuff I knew I was going to eat, so I couldn't imagine putting any kind of crazy chemicals on it. And that's pretty much why we're still doing it that way."

To keep up with the constant weeding that comes with growing organically, Dave has family members, including nieces and nephews, help out on the farm during the busiest times or when a lot of hand labor is required for harvesting. Digging out garlic is one such task. Dave plants his garlic the first week of November, when he's sure that it won't get too warm and the garlic will send roots down rather than green shoots up. He puts down a foot of straw prevent weeds. It's so effective, he says, he never has to weed once.

Last year he grew seven varieties of garlic, though he was only selling three or four. Because garlic seed is so expensive, instead of selling the first year or two of harvestable bulbs, he replants them to grow his crop, until he has enough to start selling. When it does show up to the market, Dave sells it for $1.50 a head.

Some customers grumble because they see garlic priced at 5-for-$1 at the grocery store, but Dave says the garlic he grows is drastically different than the conventional variety sold in the store. Soft-necked garlic is most common, with around 18 cloves per head. The hard-necked varieties he grows—like the Persian Star or Georgian Fire—have anywhere from four to six monster-sized cloves. The chefs like them because they require less peeling, and therefore less work. "Some people think garlic is garlic, but it's so different," Dave says.

Left: Heads of Georgian Fire garlic at Green City Market, where Dave and Denise also sell their big sunflowers. Right: Dave harvesting garlic on the farm; brilliant beans at Green City Market.

Dave specializes in tomatoes and garlic but his farm also produces a good variety of peppers and onions, collard greens, lettuces, cauliflower, broccoli, Swiss chard, and cabbage. He grows about seven or eight varieties of squash, five or six varieties of cucumbers, a handful of different tomatillos, and nearly 60 varieties of tomatoes. He is always looking for something new and fun to try.

GROWING FOR CHEFS

One of Dave's earliest restaurant customers was Browntrout, and chef Sean Sanders still shops regularly at Leaning Shed. Another was Alinea, Grant Achatz's restaurant in Lincoln Park that has had a months-long wait list since it opened in 2005, and is arguably one of the country's top restaurants.

When a chef from Alinea started buying cucumbers from Dave, he wasn't familiar with the restaurant. "I had no idea," Dave says. "I told him I would stop by to eat there once I was back in the city. He said, 'You better make your reservation right now!' I went home and Googled it, and that's when I found out what it was."

"The cool thing about the market and dealing direct is that I can say, 'What would you like me to grow, and how would you like it?'" Dave says. "For farmers it's great and for the restaurant owners it's even better than great. They get what they want—not something close to what they want."

Dave says they try to grow some "funky" things that other farms may not have. He will grow small quantities; enough for a few interested chefs to buy.

A good example is a pepper he recently started growing. A market customer who always liked to try the more unusual things Dave and Denise were selling brought back—smuggled in, that is—a beautiful pepper called the *amarillo* pepper from Mexico. The pepper starts out green, turns dark purple, and then ripens to yellow.

"Last year, Andrew Zimmerman, the chef at Sepia, was in *Saveur* magazine saying one of the top ingredients of 2010 is amarillo powder, but nobody has ever had it fresh in Chicago," Dave says, excited. "I've got maybe 50 plants, so I'm not going to have tons of it. We sell to Frontera, so I told them that we have some."

Dave likes to grow specialty things for chefs, but he also likes to bring some of those more interesting things to market, like the ground cherry—a small fruit related to the tomato with a husk that makes it look very much like a small tomatillo, and with a delicious flavor that is both sweet and savory.

"Man, so many people wanted them the first year, and if I'd sold them all to chefs, no one else could have had any," Dave says. "Yeah, I want to sell them, but this isn't all about money. It's about spreading things around, and turning people onto different things."

PERFECTLY IMPERFECT TOMATOES

One of Dave's mentors is a retired tomato farmer. He is well respected and well known for his big, red tomatoes, a single variety that he sold to grocery stores. He grew it so well he even branded it.

One day Dave and Denise had 2,000 pounds of tomatoes loaded in the trailer, getting ready for Green City Market the next day. The retired tomato farmer took one look at the collection of oddly shaped, multi-hued heirloom tomatoes, and laughed. "They're split and they look ugly and they have green tops. And he says, 'What are you nuts?' He laughs at us; he doesn't get it," Dave says, laughing himself.

Later that week, the retired farmer called Dave and asked how he did at the market, Dave remembers. "I said, 'We sold almost all of them,' and he was in shock—like who the hell would want those?"

FROM THE FARMERS: Dave and Denise Dyrek

RESOURCES AND INSPIRATION

Books

The New Organic Grower by Eliot Coleman is a good book for getting started in the farming business.

The Gardener's A–Z Guide to Growing Organic Food by Tanya L.K. Denckla breaks down every crop and gives you information on growing, fighting diseases and pests, and harvesting your crops.

Heirloom: Notes from an Accidental Tomato Farmer by Tim Stark is an easy, fun read with many laughs.

Organizations

Food Alliance (foodalliance.org) promotes sustainable farming practices.

Green City Market (greencitymarket.org) assists, supports, and believes in small, sustainable, and organic farmers.

RECIPE

SLOW-ROASTED HEIRLOOM TOMATOES

We have been making this recipe since we began growing heirloom tomatoes. At the first sign of fall or a cool day, this is the first recipe we turn to.—Dave Dyrek

> 1 cup (237 mL) plus 3 tablespoons (45 mL) olive oil, divided
> 15 heirloom tomatoes
> 3–4 cloves garlic
> A few sprigs fresh oregano or thyme
> 1–3 tablespoons (15–45 mL) balsamic vinegar
> 1–3 tablespoons (15–45 mL) kosher salt
> 1–3 tablespoons (15–45 mL) sugar

1. Line a rimmed baking sheet with foil. Pour 3 tablespoons (45 mL) of the oil in the pan. Cut the tomatoes in half and place them into the pan and gently toss them in the oil. Arrange them in a single layer and turn cut sides up.

2. Thinly slice the garlic cloves and scatter them over the tomato halves. Sprinkle with the oregano, vinegar, salt, and sugar. Pour the remaining oil over the tomatoes. Bake on the center of the oven at 350°F (180°C) 3 hours. Serve warm as a side dish or on slices of baguette as an appetizer.

3. Store tomatoes, covered, in the refrigerator for up to 1 week or frozen for up 2 months; leftover oil can be refrigerated and used for vinaigrettes.

HEIRLOOM TOMATO SALAD

By **Sean Sanders**, Browntrout

4–6 SERVINGS

When Dave first started at the farmers' market, I walked in and the wind was blowing south and I could smell his tomatoes. That was one of the first things that drew me to Dave —the fact that I could smell his tomatoes from 30 feet away, and I said, "I gotta buy this guy's tomatoes."—Sean Sanders

> **Fresh cheese curds**
> **Buttermilk**
> **1 cup (121 g) all-purpose flour**
> **Coarsely ground sea salt**
> **Pepper**
> **1½ cups (80 g) sourdough bread cubes (¼-inch [6-mm] cubes)**
> **Mild extra-virgin olive oil**
> **1 cup (237 mL) vegetable oil**
> **2–3 pounds (908–1.36 kg) heirloom tomatoes**
> **Aged balsamic vinegar (choose one that is little thick and syrupy)**
> **Fresh basil leaves, torn into ½-inch (2.5-cm) pieces**

1. Cover cheese curds with buttermilk and soak right before you fry them. Place flour in a bowl, season with salt and pepper, and set aside.

2. For croutons, heat a little of the olive oil in a small skillet over medium heat. Add bread cubes, sauté until golden brown, season to taste with salt and pepper, and drain on paper towels. Set aside.

3. Heat the vegetable oil in a medium high-sided saucepan to 350°F (180°C). Drain cheese curds and coat well with the flour, shaking off any excess. Fry curds in oil about 1 minute, or until lightly golden brown. Drain on paper towels.

4. Slice tomatoes and assemble on plates. Season to taste with salt and pepper, drizzle with vinegar and olive oil. Sprinkle with basil, top with croutons and fried cheese curds, and serve immediately.

ROASTED FEDERLE TOMATO SOUP

WITH SAXON'S GREENFIELDS GRILLED CHEESE SANDWICHES

By **Andrew Zimmerman**, Sepia

4 SERVINGS

> **4 pounds (1.82 kg) fresh Federle tomatoes, cored**
> **½ cup (119 mL) extra-virgin olive oil**
> **1 bunch fresh oregano**
> **6 medium cloves garlic, peeled and cut in half**
> **Salt and pepper, to taste**
> **Softened butter as needed**
> **8 slices Red Hen Bakery Pane Francese**
> **16 slices Saxon Creamery's Greenfields Cheese**
> **¼ cup (59 mL) crème fraîche**
> **Additional olive oil**

1. To prepare the soup, cut the tomatoes into halves vertically. Place the tomatoes in a roasting pan and toss with the olive oil, oregano, garlic, and a pinch of salt and pepper. Arrange the tomatoes in a single layer. Roast the tomatoes at 375°F (190°C) until they collapse and give up some of their juices, about 30 to 40 minutes. (The tomatoes should be lightly blackened in a few spots but not burned or dried out.) If the garlic slices start to brown, remove them and reserve until the tomatoes are pureed.

2. When the tomatoes are roasted, remove the oregano stems, leaving the leaves behind. Transfer tomato mixture, in batches, to a blender and blend until smooth. Season to taste with salt and pepper. Keep the soup warm.

3. To make the sandwiches, generously butter one side of each bread slice. Arrange the cheese slices on the unbuttered sides of 4 bread slices. Top with the remaining bread slices. Preheat a skillet pan or griddle over medium-low heat and cook the sandwiches until the bread is brown and crisp and the cheese is melted.

4. Whisk the crème fraîche until it thickens. Divide the soup among 4 warmed soup bowls, top with a dollops of crème fraîche, and drizzle with olive oil. Serve the soup with the sandwiches on the side.

CHAPTER 12

PRAIRIE FRUITS FARM & CREAMERY

Wes Jarrell and Leslie Cooperband | Champaign, Illinois | prairiefruits.com

For Leslie Cooperband and Wes Jarrell, the art and science of making good goat cheese starts with the soil. "It's about the milk quality, and that starts with the animals, but first it starts with the land," Leslie says. "We grow all of our own forage, between the hay and the pasture, it's all grown right here. That has to be done well, and it has to be done so that the nutritional value is the highest possible."

At Prairie Fruits Farm and Creamery, Illinois's first farmstead creamery (though no longer the only), Leslie and Wes raise La Mancha and Nubian goats, whose rich milk is the basis of the cheeses they make on site.

When they first moved to the farm in 2003 to start raising goats and making cheese, the land had been farmed industrially, and the soil needed healing. They converted 37 acres from corn and soybeans into pastures of hay, and turned the most eroded areas into two acres of prairie restoration by putting in perennial plants and not cultivating the soil. By resting the land, "you get biology happening in the soil year round again," Wes says. "The texture is coming back too. Before, it was just like cement, it wouldn't break up. We've added quite a lot of compost to these fields."

Both Leslie and Wes have soil science backgrounds; Leslie taught at the University of Wisconsin, and then part time at the University of Illinois, where Wes was head of the Natural Resources and Environmental Sciences department. Moving to the farm was a natural transition; Leslie says there are more similarities between soil and cheese than you'd think.

"I did a lot of work with compost, and cheesemaking is like controlled decomposition or controlled fermentation," Leslie says.

THE GOATS

The cheese-making facility, where everything is clean and shiny stainless steel, is a laboratory. Leslie is a scientist, and two full-time cheesemakers work alongside her, measuring the pH of the milk and cheese at various stages, monitoring each cheese as it gets further along in the fermentation process. But when Leslie takes off her hairnet and lab coat and transitions to caring for her goats, she becomes a loving den mother.

Each of the 70-some milking goats has a name. With each group of new goats born and raised on the farm, Leslie creates a theme for their names. Like movie stars of the '30s and '40s, or gemstones and jazz singers, where the goats Ella Fitzgerald, Nina Simone, and Opal all got their names.

The bond Leslie and Wes have with the goats isn't just sentimental, it's practical. It's important that milking goats bond closely to the people who are taking care of them; with two milkings a day, they need to be approachable and relatively acquiescent. Because the kids, or baby goats, are separated from their mothers at birth, the kids bond to Leslie and Wes from the beginning. Leslie says the reason for the kids not to nurse their mothers is twofold: one, so that the goats bond to people, rather than their mothers, and two, because they believe the sooner the kid and mother are separated, the less traumatic it is on them both.

Leslie and Wes sell the male kids and keep the females as milkers. The girls are fed their mothers' milk by bottle, and eventually put out on pasture where they are rotationally grazed, meaning they move from one paddock, or enclosed field, to another each day. Grazing the goats in this way gives the pasture time to grow back after the goats have eaten it down, and it also prevents the goats from eating the forage down too low to the ground.

Leslie and Wes keep a few billies—male goats—on the farm, and breed the goats naturally. The goats are bred in the fall, they kid (give birth), in the spring, and lactate through November or December. Their goats are seasonal breeders and therefore, seasonal lactators. By the very end of their lactation cycle, the milking goes down to once a day. But during peak production, the goats are brought in from pasture twice a day to be milked.

THE CHEESE

The first of two daily milkings starts at 5:30 in the morning. The fresh milk goes into a holding tank where the temperature is brought down to 40 degrees before it is pumped two rooms over to the cheese making room. There it goes into a large vat for pasteurization. By the end of that day, cheese has been made from that day's milk.

"Milk travels about 40 feet from the time it comes out of the goat and by the time it gets made into cheese," says Wes. "It's all in stainless steel, and we think that makes it purer: along with being fresh it's also cleaner and colder, which is the secret for goat milk. If it gets dirty or warm, it breaks down and starts giving off flavors."

Once it's in the make room, the milk is vat pasteurized in two 50 gallon vats. Vat pasteurization holds the milk at 145°F (63°C) for 30 minutes; Leslie says the low temperature achieves the goal of pathogen destruction without altering the chemistry of the milk.

With cheesemaking, acidity is very important, "We measure the pH of this from the very beginning of the process all the way to the aging room," Leslie says.

Fresh chevre is Wes and Leslie's "bread and butter," and any given week, they are making it. It was the cheese they started with but they have since expanded by adding ripened goat cheese, soft ripened sheep's cheese (they buy sheep's milk from an Amish farmer 40 miles away), a couple of semi-hard cheeses, and a hard cheese, for a total of eight or nine cheeses currently in production.

Their Angel Food and Little Bloom on the Prairie (two soft-ripened, bloomy rind goat cheeses) have brilliant white rinds. Moonglo is a raw goat milk tomme-style cheese, with a rind washed in "tea" made from Moonglo pear leaves grown on the farm. Red Dawn is a brilliantly hued round of soft-ripened goat milk cheese dusted in smoked paprika.

Prairie Fruits Farm uses the sheep's milk for five of their cheeses, including two raw milk cheeses (Kaskaskia and Roxanne) and two soft-ripened cheese (Black Sheep and Ewe Bloom). Krotovina (named for a buried darkened layer in a soil profile) is a soft-ripened cheese with an ash layer separating a layer of goat milk cheese and a layer of sheep milk cheese.

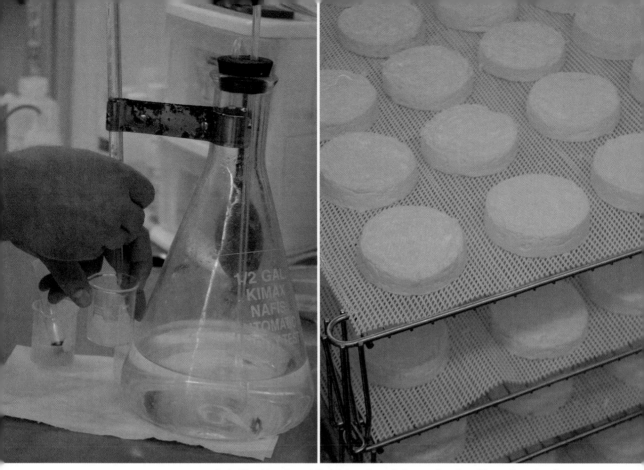

Left: Checking the acidity of the whey of chevre after the milk was inoculated.
Right: Little Bloom on the Prairie ready for the aging room.

Each style of cheese has its own aging room with differing levels of humidity. One of the bloomy rind goat cheeses, Little Bloom on the Prairie, is a cut curd camembert-style cheese with a creamy core and gooey exterior. After about a week in its aging room where a fogger keeps humidity levels high, it develops a beautiful white bloom on its exterior. It's aged for three to four weeks.

The pecorinos are aged the longest, at 12 or 13 months. Periodically Leslie and her team do an olive oil mix with black current jam that they wash the cheese in, part of the attempt to incorporate the taste and flavor of the farm into the cheese.

LINKED TO THE LAND

When Wes and Leslie moved to the farm, they began to grow certified organic tree fruits and berries, including peaches, apples, currants, gooseberries,

raspberries, and blackberries. They also have an herb and vegetable garden, and often use fresh herbs in their cheese.

By growing the forage that their goats eat, by using fruits and vegetables that they grow, Wes and Leslie hope to impart a connection of land to food essential to creating terroir-based cheeses. Terroir, the linking of food products—most often wine—to specific regions, has its roots in the European food tradition, but it is finding its way to this continent with producers like Wes and Leslie who seek to give their cheeses special characteristics that are related to their unique circumstances of geology, land, and soil.

Chefs in Chicago who use Prairie Fruits Farm cheese, may not be able to put their fingers on the why they prefer it, but just as many of these chefs are creating a cuisine based on this region of the country, using what local growers and producers provide. Leslie and Wes are creating cheese based on their region as well.

"For me, it's probably one of my favorite goat cheeses that is made anywhere in the United States," says Paul Virant, chef of Vie and Perennial Virant and a leader in the local foods movement. "It's a really high quality cheese, it's very clean, and very fresh."

FROM THE FARMERS: Wes Jarrell | Leslie Cooperband

RESOURCES AND INSPIRATION

Books: ***Blessed Are the Cheesemakers*** by Sarah-Kate Lynch, ***Goat Song*** by Brad Kessler, ***The Omnivore's Dilemma*** by Michael Pollan, ***Goatkeeping 101***

Journals: ***Dairy Goat Journal***, ***Culture***

Online: **attra.org**; **dairyfoodsconsulting.com**; **smalldairy.com**

RECIPE

GOAT CHEESE AND PRODUCE FRITTATA

4 SERVINGS

- **6 to 8 eggs**
- **1 cup (237 mL) whole milk**
- **1 small onion, chopped**
- **1 tablespoon (15 mL) olive oil**
- **About 1 cup (150 g) chopped seasonal local vegetables, such as leeks, mushrooms, Roma tomatoes, kale, or chard**
- **Salt and pepper**
- **½ to 2/3 of a 6-ounce (170-g) container of Prairie Fruits Farm Chevre**
- **½ cup (50 g) grated Prairie Fruits Farm pecorino cheese or shredded Moonglo cheese**
- **Several pinches of smoked paprika**

1. Whisk eggs together with milk in a large bowl. Sauté the onion in oil in a large ovenproof skillet over medium heat about 2 minutes. Add the chopped vegetables and sauté until soft. Add egg mixture and season with salt and pepper. Cook and stir the egg mixture briefly, then add the chevre in dollops. Sprinkle with the pecorino cheese.

2. Cook without stirring until the egg mixture is set on the bottom but still soft and a little runny on top. Dust with paprika.

3. Place the frittata under a broiler preheated on high and broil just until set and golden brown on top. Cool slightly, cut into wedges, and serve with a salad of local greens and lightly toasted artisanal bread.

INDIVIDUAL GOAT CHEESECAKES

By **Bruce Sherman**, North Pond

4–6 SERVINGS

> 1 teaspoon powdered gelatin
>
> 4 teaspoons cold water
>
> 4 ounces (114-g) fresh chevre/goat's milk cheese, preferably Prairie Fruit Farms
>
> 2 tablespoons sugar
>
> ½ vanilla bean, scraped
>
> Lemon zest, to taste
>
> ¼ cup (59 mL) heavy cream, whipped to soft peaks

1. Line 4 to 6 (2-inch [5-cm]) ramekins with plastic wrap and set aside.

2. Spinkle the gelatin on top of the water and let stand 3 to 5 minutes or until softened. Warm a small portion of the goat cheese in a small saucepan over low heat and dissolve the gelatin in it. Combine the remaining cheese, sugar, vanilla, and lemon zest in a bowl. Stir in the warm cheese mixture. Fold in the whipped cream.

3. Portion into prepared ramekins and place in refrigerator 4 to 12 hours until set. Carefully unwrap. Serve with strawberries or rhubarb jam.

MOSCATO GOAT CHEESECAKE

By **Paul Virant and Elissa Narow**, pastry chef, Perennial Virant

> 1½ cups (182 g) all-purpose flour
>
> ¼ teaspoon salt
>
> ½ cup (100 g) plus 2 tablespoons sugar
>
> 7 ounces (199 g) cold unsalted butter, cubed
>
> 8 ounces (227 g) cream cheese, softened
>
> 8 ounces (227 g) Praire Fruits Farm fresh chevre, softened
>
> 1 cup (200 g) sugar
>
> Pinch of salt
>
> 4 eggs
>
> ¼ cup (25 mL) moscato wine

1. Preheat oven to 350°F (180°C).

2. To prepare crust, place flour, sugar, and salt in a food processor. Add butter and blend until mixture resembles coarse cornmeal. Press into an 8-inch (20-cm) springform pan. Bake until light golden brown. Cool crust. Reduce oven temperature to 300°F (150°C).

3. Cream cheeses with sugar and salt with an electric mixer just until smooth. Add the eggs, one at a time, beating after each addition. Beat in the wine just until blended. Do not overmix. Pour filling over the crust. Bake in a waterbath until set but slightly jiggly in the center. Cool completely. Serve chilled with Concord Grape Sauce (page 101).

CHAPTER 13

SEEDLING ORCHARD

Peter Klein | South Haven, Michigan | seedlingfruit.com

O n a breezy day in June, Peter Klein's first pineberry is ripe. Or he thinks it is. It's hard to tell, because pineberries are a white strawberry with red seeds that seem to be ripe when they have a just a hint of blush on their fair skin. It is Peter's first year growing them, at the request of chef Meg Galus at NoMI Kitchen, at the Park Hyatt Chicago, and he's not sure what to expect.

He takes his first bite and behind his sunglasses, his entire face explodes into a smile. "Oh my God, it's delicious!"

The story Peter likes to tell of how he first came into farming is this: His favorite fruit guys at his local Chicago farmers' market were selling their Michigan fruit orchard. The idea got planted in his head to buy it, though he hadn't farmed a day in his life. A year later, unable to shake the idea, he visited the farm, fell in love with it, and put together a business plan. Peter looked at the bottom line and decided it was a bad idea. A really bad idea. And then he quit his job and bought it.

THE LAND

Seedling Orchard is in South Haven, Michigan. It's a beautiful 81 acres of land lush with fruit trees spread across the gently rolling hills dotted with wild flowers, all the idyllic backdrop to a turn-of-the-century farmhouse. It's not hard to see why Peter became enamored; it's really pretty.

With the purchase of the orchard, Peter inherited many of the trees that still provide him with his current crops: the pear, apple, cherry, and peach trees. He was also blessed with the good fortune of having the previous owners relocate across the street, where they have served as a helpful resource. Using guidance from his neighbors, know-how from his foreman (who had been living on the property for more than 10 years), and his laid-back, happy-go-lucky sort of approach, Peter started planting and trying, learning and playing.

Fewer than 10 years after he bought the orchard, Seedling has become a weekly fixture at five markets across Chicago, where people crowd around in the summer to buy his fruit smoothies, popsicles, jams, farmstead cider, and of course, fresh fruit. Peter also shows up with Seedling to a lot of events throughout the city, from the monthly Dose Market, a stylish new market concept featuring local vendors in food and fashion, to Chipotle's Cultivate event in Lincoln Park, highlighting local Midwest producers and farmers.

People are as attracted to Seedling's fruit as they are to Peter's personality, which is charming and easy, sweet and sarcastic. He has a constant sense of humor, and a laid-back attitude that helps when you're growing fruit in southwest Michigan. He is willing to try to grow just about anything, with the possibility that something won't work out. Right now, in addition to apples, pears,

peaches, and cherries, his orchard is home to elderberries, huckleberries, gooseberries, figs, currants, and goji berries. Fraises des bois, strawberries, blueberries, ground cherries, and a variety of melons show up on his market tables when they're in season; quince trees, persimmon, medlar, and pawpaw trees are new additions to the farm in the last couple of years.

FARMING PRACTICES

Because of the moisture in the Midwest, it's hard to grow fruit organically. Peter employs a system called Integrated Pest Management. To track everything, he hired a scout who comes to the orchard weekly, sets traps, counts bugs, looks for problems, and helps figure out how to handle them.

"I don't care so much if it's not perfect," Peter says. "If you're selling everything you can to the wholesalers, you really have to chemical it. But if we make jams, imperfect fruit is okay."

Most of Peter's Michigan neighbors are large-scale growers, like the cucumber farm nearby that mechanically harvests cucumbers for grocery stores and major retailers like Walmart, who require a specific size and shape.

"If it has a curve, too big, too short—they toss. They throw out a semi load every day," Peter says. "That's what happens with the big fruit growers, too. Anything that is too small gets composted. By hand-picking, we can totally avoid that. Maybe a machine will go through it once. We go through four or five times. If a machine picker goes through and gets a bunch of unripe ones, they just toss them."

With the time and care that Peter and his crew dedicate to harvesting every crop by hand, it's easy to understand that he bristles at the thought of wasting any of it because of an imperfect shape or a mild bruise.

"Value added is so important to me because I don't want to waste any of this," he says. "Composting is good, but I'd rather make it into a product."

If Peter has fruit from the market he doesn't sell, then it goes to the jam maker, or into Seedling's sorbets, popsicles, or smoothies.

Seedling currently has about 28 different varieties of apples. They try to do a lot of varieties, so when a crop is ready to harvest, they don't suddenly

have to hand pick 200,000 pounds at once. And, Peter says, the beauty of the cider mill is that you don't have to harvest when it's harvest time, you can just let the apples hang, and they just develop more sugar and more flavor to be used for cider.

COLLABORATING WITH CHEFS

Spend about five minutes with Peter and you'll quickly learn that he's a connector who loves to collaborate with people. Amid all of his pear, apple, and cherry trees, his fields of melons and blueberries and more, what gets him the most excited are the small, specialty fruits he plays with, and the collaborations with chefs and local companies, like the pineberries he's growing for Meg Galus, or the cherries grown exclusively for Goose Island for a cherry-infused beer.

A recent collaboration with Carrie Nahabedian of Naha went especially well. "Last year, Peter asked me, 'Is there anything you want me to grow for you?'" Carrie says. "As a lark, I sent him a picture of the pears in the bottle for Poire Williams and said, 'Do you think you could do this?'"

Peter had his carefree approach to the challenge. "She called me up and said, 'Hey, can you grow pear in a bottle?' and I said, 'I don't know, let's find out!'" Peter hung 24 bottles on his pear trees on wired branches where pears would grow, and 20 survived. Carrie had Ravenswood-based Koval brandy do an apple and a pear brandy with the bottled pears, and special labels designed by her architect brother. Customers and restaurant staffers alike were excited, press followed, and Peter did it again the next year.

"That's the fun part of this business, the partnerships. It's not just, 'Hey I grow peaches and whatever I have left I sell to Gerber and they make it into baby food.'" Peter says. "That's not exciting. Growing delicious fruits is exciting. The partnerships—really creating stuff—to me that's what's really interesting."

"We picked green strawberries for chefs. They're not ripe, totally disgusting, but chefs think it's cool. They love to pickle them, or use them in a simple syrup. They don't really taste like strawberries but they have some acidity. We did it for two restaurants (Blackbird and Custom House) last year and we have like 10 orders this year."

Peter has a long list of good relationships with chefs across the city, from places like Topolobampo and Lula Cafe, to the Elysian and Trump hotels. He has clients like Google, which stocks its Chicago office cafeteria with Seedling fruit, as well as mixologists like Tim Lacey at The Drawing Room and Mike Ryan at Sable, who love to use Peter's products in their drinks. Because chefs and bartenders are excited to work with new and unusual products, Peter has the liberty to play around and try growing new things, like goji berries.

What does a fresh goji berry taste like?

"I don't know, we're gonna find out!" Peter says, grinning. "I don't know anyone who has had a fresh goji berry, but I got eight last year. Eight goji berries."

And what does a medlar taste like?

"I don't know. We'll find out! Yeah. So I waste some time and money."

Like the sunberry. Peter found it in a catalogue and it looked really good. It was developed by a famous fruitologist who called it a *wonderberry*, comparing it to a small blueberry but with better flavor. Peter ordered it and grew it. "It was nasty," he says. "It was almost inedible, like a savory berry."

But some of the mishaps turn into successes. Peter planted 10 elderberry bushes only to discover that the berries weren't good to eat, but that chefs love the flowers. So he planted another 20 to 30 bushes, and started taking pre-orders for flowers.

"It's about the product, the fruit, and what can you grow that is fun and interesting," Peter says. "That is one of the things that is so exciting about it to me."

Peter takes another pineberry bite and pulls out his phone. "I have to call Meg. She's gotta know how good these are."

Below: Seedling's cider mill is ready for sugar-dense apples. Right: Peter amid the wildflower and pear trees on his orchard.

FROM THE FARMER: Peter Klein

RESOURCES AND INSPIRATION

For me it was really about the food itself: growing, using, eating the best-tasting food, which eventually led me to thinking that the more local food is, the better. Those products, if grown right, have so much more flavor than shipped varieties. You can let them ripen properly, you can grow varieties that don't ship, and get great product. The book that most inspired me for this was *The Herbfarm Cookbook* by Jerry Traunfeld.

It turns out that I am inspired by the nature aspect of the whole thing. Wandering through trees, enjoying the quiet or the sounds of nature and animals. I find that time to be totally refreshing and restoring. My inspiration: *Flat Rock Journal: A Day in the Ozark Mountains* by Ken Carey. Beware, this is a total new age masterpiece!

FREE FORM APPLE TART

4–6 SERVINGS

> **All-Butter Pie Crust (recipe follows)**
> **1 quart (440 g) apples**
> **4 tablespoons (57 g) unsalted butter**
> **2 tablespoons granulated sugar**
> **1 tablespoon melted butter**
> **2 tablespoons packed brown sugar**

1. Prepare All-Butter Pie Crust.

2. Peel, core, and cut each apple into 16 slices. Preheat oven to 400°F (200°C).

3. Melt the butter in a large skillet over medium heat. Sauté the apples with the granulated sugar until crisp-tender and golden, stirring occasionally.

4. While the apples are cooking, roll out the pie crust dough on a lightly floured surface to a ⅛-inch-thick (3-mm) circle. Top with apples, leaving the outer 1 inch (2.5 cm) of the dough uncovered. Fold the edge of the dough over the apples, pleating it as needed. Brush dough with melted butter, sprinkle the entire tart with brown sugar. Bake 25 minutes, or until the crust is golden brown.

ALL-BUTTER PIE CRUST

> **1 cup (121 g) all-purpose flour**
> **2 teaspoons sugar**
> **1 teaspoon salt**
> **7 tablespoons (100 g) unsalted butter, cubed**
> **3 tablespoons (45 mL) ice water**

1. Place the flour, sugar, and salt in a food processor. Process briefly. Add the butter and pulse about a dozen times until the butter is in pea-sized pieces. With the machine running, add the ice water and process until the mixture begins to form a ball. Shape the dough into a disk, wrap in plastic wrap, and chill at least 1 hour.

SEEDLING ORCHARD APPLE SALAD

By **Randy Zweiban**, Province

4—6 SERVINGS

> 4 cups (440 g) julienned apples, such as Honey Crisp or Gala
> 3 cups (360 g) peeled and julienned jicama
> ¾ cup (178 mL) Candied Olives (recipe follows)
> ¼ cup (12 g) finely chopped chives
> ¾ cup (107 g) Marcona almonds, toasted, chopped
> ½ cup (119 mL) Seedling Apple Cider Vinaigrette (recipe follows)
> 1 tablespoon kosher salt
> 1 tablespoon freshly toasted and ground black pepper

1. Prepare Candied Olives and Seedling Apple Cider Vinaigrette.

2. Toss the apples, jicama, candied olives, and chives together in a large bowl. Add some of the vinaigrette and toss to coat. Add the nuts and season the salad with the salt and pepper. Plate the salad and drizzle some of the vinaigrette around the plates.

CANDIED OLIVES

> 1 cup (227 g) water
> 1 cup (200 g) sugar
> ¾ cup (101 g) Arbequina and Coquille olives, pitted

1. Boil water and sugar until the sugar dissolves, stirring constantly.

2. Remove from the heat and cool to about 170°F (80°C). Pour over olives in a bowl. Cool to room temperature. Let the olives stand about 15 minutes, then strain, and chop them.

SEEDLING APPLE CIDER VINAIGRETTE

> 2 cups (474 mL) Seedling apple cider
> 1 cup (237 mL) olive oil
> ¼ cup (59 mL) champagne vinegar
> Kosher salt and freshly toasted and ground black pepper

1. Heat the apple cider in a small saucepan to simmering. Simmer until the cider is reduced to about 1 cup (237 mL). Whisk in the vinegar and season to taste with salt and toasted pepper. Cool.

PEAR AND GINGER HAND PIES

By **Jason Hammel**, Lula Cafe

16 SERVINGS

3⅔ (443 g) cups all-purpose flour

2 tablespoons (30 mL) granulated sugar

1 teaspoon (5 mL) salt

10½ ounces (298 g) cold unsalted butter, cubed

1 egg, cold

About ¼ cup (57 g) ice water

3 to 4 firm ripe pears, such as Anjou, peeled, chopped into ¼-inch (6-mm) pieces

1½ teaspoon (7.5 mL) candied ginger, chopped into ⅛-inch (3-mm) pieces

¼ cup (56 g) packed light brown sugar

2 tablespoons (30 mL) crème fraîche or sour cream

1 egg

Demerara sugar (optional)

1. Combine the flour, granulated sugar, salt, and butter in the bowl of a stand mixer. Using the paddle attachment, mix on the lowest speed until the butter is in pea-sized pieces. With the mixer running, add the egg and mix until blended. Add the ice water, 1 tablespoon at a time, mixing just until the dough looks shaggy and feels slightly wet. Knead the dough briefly on a floured surface and form into a disk. Wrap in plastic wrap and refrigerate about 30 minutes.

2. Roll out the dough on a lightly floured surface to ³/₁₆-inch (5-mm) thickness and cut out 4-inch (10 cm) rounds. Use the scraps to roll out again, if desired. You should have about 16 rounds. Cover and chill while making the filling.

3. To prepare the filling, combine the pears, brown sugar, and crème fraîche, and ginger in a bowl and gently fold the ingredients together.

4. Place a heaping tablespoon of the filling onto the center of each disk. Whisk the egg and brush around half of each dough circle. Fold each dough circle in half over the filling and crimp the edge with a fork. Place on a baking sheet and chill at least 1 hour.

5. Preheat the oven to 350°F (180°C). Brush the surface of each pie with the egg wash, cut 3 slits as vents, and sprinkle with the demerara sugar. Bake about 45 minutes, or until golden brown. Serve warm or at room temperature.

CHAPTER 14

THREE SISTERS GARDEN

Tracey Vowell and Kathe Roybal | Kankakee, Illinois

Tracey Vowell and Kathe Roybal met David Wulff the first year they started farming, in 2000, after they put an ad in the farm bureau paper asking for help with turning their soil. "David was the only person who responded, and we got really, really lucky," Tracey says.

It's an unexpected relationship: two small-scale growers new to farming and trying to do it sustainably, and one seasoned professional farmer, who houses more than a dozen John Deere tractors and farms commodity corn and soybeans on 2,000 acres.

"It's been interesting. Most people think, 'You're a sustainable, organic farmer, so the big guys are the devil,'" Tracey says. "Well, yes and no. The big guys know a lot of stuff, and they have a lot of equipment. And our big guy is a really helpful and unique individual."

"Verdolagas was one of the very first things we did with him," says Tracey, referring to a wild green, commonly called *purslane*, that chefs like to cook with and that most large-scale farmers consider a weed. "Once he got over the fact that you could actually make cold hard cash cuttin' down your weeds, we had his attention."

Then she told him, "I just happen to know a place where we can sell thousands of beans, if we can produce them.'"

FROM CHEFS TO FARMERS

Tracey was the managing chef at Frontera Grill, where Kathe was also working, when they fell in love with the idea of moving to a farm. They were on a tour of a farm in Plainfield, Illinois, with the Frontera Farmer Foundation. They asked the farmers who lived in the house on the farm, and they said, "Oh, just a renter." And Tracey told them, "If your just-a-renter happens to just-a-leave, give us a call."

Six months later, the renters left; Tracey and Kathe moved in. They had one full season on that farm before Tracey and Kathe started looking for their own piece of land. In 2000, they purchased their nine-acre property in Kankakee County.

Tracey continued to work at Frontera when they first started Three Sisters Garden, working part-time on the farm. Five years later, she quit and moved to Kankakee to farm full time with Kathe.

"Farming for someone who is coming at it like we are is just a giant mystery tour," Tracey says. "We are in our 12th season, and every year, something just completely mind boggling happens. It might be a whole lot of water, or a really dry summer, or a lot of really tenacious weeds, or a bug we never saw."

They say David, who grew up on a farm and to whom farming is second nature, has been essential to helping with each new problem that arises. One

year, after driving by and seeing the corn Tracey had planted, David called her on the phone and said, "Tracey, you planted your corn too close together—go crawl through your corn and rip out every other plant." Kathe starts to laugh a little, remembering. Tracey shakes her head. "Oh it was awful. That was five years ago. But we did it, and sure enough, we had a good harvest," she says. "And the little scrap of a patch where we decided to leave it just to see? Not an ear of corn. Not one."

They call David when their tractor won't run, or when they need help getting their fields ready to plant. He does all of their big tractor work—clearing their field so that it's ready to plant. They also raise a lot of their vegetable crops on his soil, where he can keep an eye on them. He has a crew of workers who help hand weed the rows.

It took a couple of years, but he became open to the idea: "David got to the point where he was like 'Yeah, these two crazy women, they just don't know anything, but it seems like they do know how to move some produce, and they do have a clear idea on what they need to be producing,'" Tracey says. "We came with all of the stuff that was really mysterious to him."

They started their farm business with two ideas in mind. "How do we go all year round, instead of being someone who disappears for half the year? And two, let's grow things that are hard to get or are in short supply already," Tracey says. "So we tend to focus on weird things and we have this really freaky crop list—but it works for us."

Tracey and Kathe grow edible flowers, including bachelor buttons, marigolds, snapdragons, Queen Anne's lace, and lily buds—an unusual edible flower that they harvest before it blooms. The flavor of the bud is like a mild green onion without the heat. Kathe says chef Sarah Stegner likes to tempura batter and deep fry them; chef Bruce Sherman stuffs them with a white cheese.

Tracey and Kathe also began to focus on the things that could take them through the winter: microgreens, pea shoots, and a petite greens mix, all of which they can grow in their greenhouse; dried goods, like black beans and cornmeal; and a small selection of vegetables that weren't too labor intensive, like squash and pumpkins that store well and could be sold past peak harvest. Beans, corn, and squash, the *three sisters*, were the main agricultural crops of Native Americans, and the name Tracey and Kathe gave to their farm.

BEANS, CORN, AND SQUASH

"The black beans were the first thing," Tracey says. "I knew where we could sell a lot of black beans, and I knew there was not a lot of competition, particularly in large quantities. That kicked the door open for thinking about what other kinds of things can we play with."

As managing chef at Frontera, Tracey spent time looking for local black beans, as well as locally produced flour and cornmeal.

"One of the things we found when we started doing it was that cornmeal that was just ground in the last few days is a whole lot better than cornmeal

that is ground once a year and stored," she says. "The idea that dry goods are completely stable just simply isn't true."

Tracey and Kathe say the first time they rolled oats, they realized that all they had ever eaten in their lifetime were rancid oats. "You know when you open the box, and you get that sweet sour cardboard smell? That's what rancid oats smell like," Tracey says. "Ours don't smell like that. Ours smell sweet, nutty, and rich, and we work really hard to make sure it stays that way."

They grind their corn and roll their oats once a week and are careful not to store them for long after, so that their dried goods are always fresh. "It upsets some of our chef accounts sometimes," Tracey says, "when they call at 7 p.m. and they need 30 pounds of coarse cornmeal the next day, and I say, 'I'm really sorry but I don't have 30 pounds ground, I have 10 for tomorrow, and we'll bring the rest to you on Friday.'"

Along with the white corn Tracey and Kathe grow for their coarse- and fine-grind cornmeals, they grow sweet corn, yellow popcorn, and white popcorn. They sell the popcorn on ears and bulk in bags.

Each corn is a different variety, and the way it grows determines its best-intended use. The white corn has really big kernels that dry well for grinding. With popcorn, the kernels are really small, and the skin on each kernel is particularly tough. When heat is applied, the last little bit of moisture that is in the kernel turns to steam and starts to expand, but the skin is so tough that the pressure really builds before it rips open, and that is what allows it to puff. Sweet corn has a lot of sugar, and it's not useful when dry, except as seed.

"We grow an exceptionally good variety of sweet corn, it's a little bit delicate and more difficult to grow, and our ears aren't as big," Tracey says. "But you can confidently pick up any old ear, say to someone, 'Peel it back, and have a taste,' and watch them proceed to eat the whole ear off and then buy a whole sackful. We like to take that approach—be careful of what you grow, and no matter if you had your game on or not, when you get there, they want it."

As for the squash and pumpkins, they grow a variety, including some just for Sarah Stegner at Prairie Grass Cafe.

A lot of Kathe and Tracey's relationships with chefs were formed when they themselves were chefs in the city, and on occasion they still find a way back in the kitchen.

"I've done a few events with Sarah, which are fun because I get to cook and I get to use my produce," Tracey says. "It's cool to know that you planted the seed, you watered it, you brought it along, you cut it, you bagged it, you brought it to the city, you took it out, you cooked it, and it went to the table. That's pretty groovy as far as I'm concerned."

FROM THE FARMERS: Tracey Vowell | Kathe Roybal

RESOURCES AND INSPIRATION

Michael Pollan was one of our biggest influences regarding getting into farming, and becoming more concerned about food and the environment, and developing an understanding of how things have gone so terribly wrong regarding commercial agriculture.

Our other biggest resources have turned out to be **other farmers in Illinois and Wisconsin** who have opened their farms to us for visits, acted as consultants, and pointed us in better directions as our learning process has developed. We are deeply thankful to those who have been so informative and supportive to our initial efforts as beginning farmers, and in the ongoing development of both our farm and our approach to sustainability.

RECIPE

EASY POLENTA

4–6 SERVINGS

> 5 cups (1.19 L) liquid, stock, water, or milk
> 2 tablespoons unsalted butter
> 1¼ cups (200 g) cornmeal (coarse, fine, or a mix of the two)
> Salt, to taste

1. Heat liquid and butter to boiling in a large ovenproof saucepan. Reduce the heat to medium and slowly stir in the cornmeal. Continue to cook, stirring frequently, until thickened, 5 to 7 minutes. Cover the pan and bake at 300°F (150°C), 30 to 40 minutes, stirring every 10 minutes, or until the cornmeal is tender and the polenta is almost stiff. Season to taste with salt.

2. For more flavor, add shredded cheese, crisply cooked and crumbled bacon, or green garlic. Coconut milk can be substituted for all or part of the liquid for a subtle Asian flavor; it's especially nice with a dash or two of cayenne pepper.

STOVETOP CORNBREAD

By **Paul Fehribach**, Big Jones

MAKES 1 (10-INCH [25-CM]) OR 2 (7-INCH [17.5-CM]) ROUNDS

"I asked farm forager Mark Psilos if he knew about anywhere to get grits, and he put me in touch with Tracey. Tracey turned out to be a great person and a great resource in addition to making cornmeal that just knocks my socks off."—Paul Fehribach

3 cups (480 g) finely ground white corn meal

2 teaspoons cream of tartar

1 teaspoon baking soda

1 teaspoon salt, or more to taste

1 jalapeño pepper, seeded, minced

4 eggs

3 cups (711 mL) buttermilk

½ cup (114 g) clarified butter, fresh lard, or bacon fat

1. Combine the cornmeal, cream of tartar, baking soda, and salt in a medium bowl and mix well. In a large bowl, beat the eggs, then whisk in the buttermilk until blended. Stir in the cornmeal mixture just until dry ingredients are moistened.

2. Place butter in a 10-inch (25-cm) or 2 (7-inch [17.5-cm]) cast iron skillets heat over medium heat until hot and just beginning to smoke. Immediately, pour about half the butter into the batter and stir until blended, leaving the other half in the skillet. Pour the batter into skillet. Cover and reduce heat to low. Cook about 30 minutes, or until the bottom is very crispy, the center is very creamy and almost custard-like. Remove from heat and cool, uncovered, 10 to 15 minutes before cutting into wedges and serving hot from the skillet.

HEIRLOOM LUXURY PIE PUMPKIN SOUP
By **Sarah Stegner and George Bumbaris**, Prarie Grass Cafe
4–6 SERVINGS

    3 cups (348 g) seeded peeled pumpkin cut into chunks
    ½ cup (75 g) chopped onion
    3 sprigs thyme
    2 bay leaves
    Salt
    2 tablespoons olive oil
    8 cups (1.90 L) chicken stock
    ½ cup (119 mL) heavy cream

1. Sauté the pumpkin, onion, thyme, bay leaves, and salt in oil over medium heat until the onion is transparent. Do not let the vegetables brown.

2. Add the stock, heat to boiling, reduce heat, and simmer until the stock is reduced by ¼ and the pumpkin is tender. Stir in the cream and simmer another 5 minutes. Remove from the heat, discard the thyme and bay leaves, and blend with an immersion blender until smooth. Serve hot with toasted pumpkin seeds and popcorn.

THREE SISTERS GARDEN
KANKAKEE ILLINOIS

PART	15	**Caveny Farm**
	16	**Genesis Growers**
	17	**Shooting Star Farm**

GROWING A FARM

A rtisanal agriculture displays the intentions and approach of the fatherly farmer. Some farmers learn this over time by evolving a family farm (see Part 1) and others may have run towards this knowledge with virgin wonderment (see Part 2). There is a third group of farmers, who blend that life-long passion with self-taught awareness. This group has grown their farms slowly, building on a sense of community and a deep connection to the soil.

15

16

17

CHAPTER **15**

CAVENY FARM

John and Connie Caveny | Monticello, Illinois | cavenyfarm.com

I tell people that it's the best turkey they will ever eat, and most people think I'm crazy until they try it." John Caveny had been farming for several decades when he read an article in the paper that Slow Food Chicago was looking for a new turkey vendor.

"I called up co-leader Portia Belloc Lowndes and said, 'I think I could raise turkeys for you.' She said okay, so we started in 2002 with these Bourbon Red heritage turkeys and we've been at it ever since," John says.

TASTY TURKEYS

That first year, John and Connie raised 120 turkeys on their farm in Monticello, Illinois. Each following year they doubled the number until they reached 720 turkeys, which is the current capacity for their breeder house.

The Cavenys sell out of turkeys each year, through chef-clients in the city like Paul Virant of Vie in Western Springs and Perennial Virant in Lincoln Park, and Patrick Sheerin, of Trenchermen (and former chef at the Signature Room at the 95th); and through returning customers who order their Thanksgiving Day birds online to be picked up at one of four pickup points the weekend before Thanksgiving.

"Last year we were at the Geneva pickup point, it was cold, late in the day on Sunday," says Connie. "We start loading Friday night, and we have lots of cold, heavy birds, so by Sunday night at Geneva, we're starting to wind down. A woman approached us and said, 'Why should I buy one of your birds?' We just stood there and thought, 'Oh do we have to do this right now?' But the guy behind her said, 'It's the best bird you'll ever eat—buy one. If you don't like it I'll pay for it.' He did the sales pitch for us right there—it was amazing!"

LOCALLY GROWN **209**

John and Connie attribute the undeniably delicious flavor of their turkeys to a few key factors, including the Bourbon Red breed.

"The heritage breeds are birds that were commonly eaten before the advent of confined feeding operations, so they don't do well in confinement and they're not very efficient gainers compared to the modern genetics," says John. "But the big difference is the flavor, the texture of the meat, and the texture of the skin are so much better."

Through natural selection Bourbon Reds were the most developed of any of the heritage breeds before the Broad Breasted turkeys took over, John says.

The flavor is also attributed to the life span of the bird, which is much longer than a conventional turkey. Caveny turkeys are at least six months old by the time they're ready to harvest (industrially raised turkeys are usually slaughtered between 14 and 18 weeks old). John and Connie receive day-old poults in the mail the first week of April, and they start to process them the last week in October.

"But by doing it that way, we have a bird that is six or six-and-a-half months old, so it's reached optimal size and flavor, and it hasn't started to get tough yet," John says.

Finally, John says the way the birds are raised and what they are fed ensures a tasty turkey. In addition to a diet of locally bought corn and soybeans, Caveny turkeys peck away for bugs and grass in the rich pastures of the farm. Housed in 10 x 12-feet A-frame bottomless pens, the turkeys have plenty of room to move around and even roost in the rafters.

"Turkeys stay in flocks," John says. "They're not scattered out over 40 acres, so they might as well be in these pens where they are safe from predators, as long as you move them every day." Moving them every day means disconnecting their water source, jacking up each of the nine pens one at time and pulling them by hand on carts. Google *Caveny Farm*, zoom in on the satellite view, and you'll see a patchwork pattern that looks like tiny brown stamps in the grass (rectangle outlines left in the grass from where the turkeys have pecked it down)—satellite proof that John and Connie move their turkeys every day.

John and Connie move their turkey pens every day using hand carts so the birds will have fresh grass to peck.

HERITAGE BREEDS

In addition to turkeys, John and Connie also raise Rouen ducks, American Buff geese, and Catan sheep.

"We have to have sheep here, because we have a lot of fertilizer so we can grow a lot of grass, and well, we have to have something that eats the grass," John says.

The turkeys are seasonal, and raising other animals lets John and Connie sell past Thanksgiving. Their ducks and geese are available from Thanksgiving through Christmas; the lambs are ready by February.

"Everything we raise, we like to eat," John says. "And we have found that if we like to eat it, a lot of other people like to eat it too."

That's a pretty safe bet. By mid-October, Vie Restaurant had already purchased 200 of the 400 Rouen ducks quacking about on the pasture.

Rouen is a heritage breed of duck that chefs are known to love for its flavor. The American Buff is a rare breed of goose, included in Slow Food USA's Ark of Taste, a catalogue of heritage foods in danger of extinction. The Ark of Taste encourages sustainable production of these foods for consumption, to foster and preserve biodiversity. Small farms like Caveny contribute to maintaining this animal as part of the country's food culture.

The geese move about in a tight flock throughout the pasture, squawking and flapping their wings as they move around.

"They really don't have such a bad life," John says. "And on the last day, it's a short day."

"We could be certified organic except for the feed, which we buy locally and know where the corn comes from," John says. "Every year we do a survey and ask our customers if they want these birds raised organically, and they say no, because the cost per pound would be more. The whole thing is, know your farmer and know how the animals are taken care of."

GROWING ENERGY

Raising heritage breeds of animals on pasture is not the only effort that John and Connie make toward sustainable agriculture.

Left: American Buff geese traveling tightly together across the fields. Right: Miscanthus gigantus towers above John Caveny.

"All we grow on this farm is grass," John says. "It's either grass for animals or grass for energy. We have cool season grass for the sheep, turkeys, ducks and geese. Then we have the energy grass, miscanthus giganteus. It's the energy crop of choice in Europe. It is a 100 percent sterile, high yielding, highly productive grass."

The Cavenys started growing the grass on their farm 10 years ago when their daughter Emily built a miscanthus program for the University of Illinois for her doctoral program.

"At the time, we were the first on-farm field trials of the grass in Illinois—basically the United States—and we've been at it ever since," says John. "We've now commercialized it, and someone can buy it and grow it for energy, whether they use it for themselves or whether they sell it."

John touts the multiple uses of the plant, which he says Europe has found more than 270 uses for, from mulch to composite plastics.

The pros of miscanthus are many, according to the Cavenys. It's more than a single use plant, highly productive, and environmentally safe because it's sterile—i.e., it's not an invasive weed that can spread. It takes essentially no fertilizer to grow, so there isn't the need for crop protection products or fertilizer as there is with corn. Once miscanthus is planted and taken care of, it should last more than 20 years.

Unlike solar or wind energy that displace fossil carbon, miscanthus giganteus can reduce carbon dioxide by taking it out of the air, while improving the fertility of the soil by sinking that carbon back down through the plant's roots, into the soil.

"The nice thing is that it's current carbon," adds Connie. "You're not digging up ancient carbon, you're recycling what is already in the atmosphere, and actually sinking some back into the ground with the growth of the roots."

"This country has 34 million acres of conservation reserve program, and all that ground was once in row cropping," John says. "They need to forget the whole thing, put it all back into energy crop grasses, lower the payments from the government, stimulate the sale of market, and turn those acres back into productive land—while producing a crop that's environmentally beneficial."

FROM THE FARMERS: John and Connie Caveny

RESOURCES AND INSPIRATION

Hugh Fearnley-Whittingstall's *River Cottage* series has great recipes. He has a good one called *The River Cottage Meat Book*; he is pretty candid on how animal turns into meat and gets on your plate, but it's done tastefully. We also use the old L.L. Bean *Game and Fish Cookbook* a lot. And one of our favorites is Julia Child's *Cooking at Home*.

Local Harvest (localharvest.org) does a great service to the local food business; nearly every state has a **Buy Local** campaign through its **Department of Agriculture** that serves as a great resource.

HOW TO COOK A TURKEY

We prepare our turkey like this all the time at home, and it's really simple. You cut up a turkey and season the whole turkey with celery salt and Bavarian seasoning—sprinkle it on there liberally. Put the legs, the thighs, and the wings together with two sticks of salted butter in a roasting pan in the oven at 325°F (160°C). After half an hour, start basting every 20 minutes, then after 45 minutes, put the breast in. You are going to cook the legs and the thighs longer than the breast. We recommend you don't let the breast reach higher than 155 degrees coming out the oven. You can cook an 8 to 10 pound turkey in less than an hour and a half.

We never cook a whole bird. The thing about it, you've got to have the breast cooked at the right temperature, and the legs and thighs cooked at the right temperature. So if you're looking to do a Norman Rockwell presentation for your turkey, get a big platter, spread dressing all around, put the breast on top and put the turkey back together. And, it's so much easier to cut a cooked turkey that's been cut up already.

When we cook ours, we don't cover it. It's cooked uncovered in a shallow pan, and by basting with butter, we can get that turkey to look like the cover of a magazine. It's beautiful—everything is better with butter.

We always boil the back, neck, gizzard and the heart to make a stock, and then you're going to have some pretty concentrated juice in the bottom of that roasting pan to make gravy.

CAVENY FARMS OVEN-POACHED RED BOURBON TURKEY BREAST

WITH TURKEY SAUSAGE-STUFFED RIGATONI AND CREAMED MUSHROOMS

By **Patrick Sheerin**, Trenchermen

4–6 SERVINGS

The color of the turkeys that come from Caveny is amazing, especially the leg and thigh. You can tell these birds get to run around and have a great time. This is a riff on turkey tetrazzini, something we had a lot of after Thanksgiving every year.—Patrick Sheerin

> **1 turkey breast half with skin on**
> **Salt and pepper**
> **½ pound (227 g) unsalted butter**
> **3 fresh sage leaves**
> **4 sprigs of thyme**
> **Turkey Sausage-Stuffed Rigatoni (recipe follows)**
> **Mushroom Cream Sauce (recipe follows)**
> **Chopped parsley**

1. Liberally season both the skin and flesh side of breast with salt and pepper. Melt the butter in a small saucepan and add the sage and thyme. Place butter in a high-sided oval non-reactive baking pan that the turkey breast will barely fit in. Carefully place the turkey breast into the pan, pushing down gently so the butter comes up over the edges of the meat. Place a probe thermometer set at 145°F (63°C) into the thickest part of the breast, and bake the turkey at 200°F (100°C) oven until it its internal temperature reaches 145°F (63°C), about 3 to 4 hours.

2. Prepare Turkey Sausage-Stuffed Rigatoni and Mushroom Cream Sauce.

3. Remove the turkey from the oven, let it rest 30 minutes at room temperature. Meanwhile, increase the oven temperature to 450°F (240°C). Place the turkey on a rack and place in the oven for 10 minutes until the skin is crisp and golden brown. Remove from the oven and let it rest for at least 10 minutes before slicing.

4. To serve, place the rigatoni on plates and top with sliced turkey breast. Garnish with parsley.

TURKEY SAUSAGE-STUFFED RIGATONI

1 pound (454 g) skinless, boneless turkey dark meat, cut into 1-inch (2.5-cm) pieces, chilled

Salt

2 large egg whites

1½ cups (356 mL) heavy cream

Fine chiffonade of flat-leaf parsley

Finely chopped tarragon

Pinch of freshly ground white pepper

Pinch cayenne pepper

5–7 rigatoni per person, cooked al dente

1. Place the turkey and a pinch of salt in a food processor and pulse until the turkey is finely chopped. Add the egg whites and pulse until smooth. With the machine running, add the cream in a steady stream and process until smooth. Scrape this mousse into a bowl and stir in the parsley, tarragon, and peppers. Transfer the mousse to a heavy-duty gallon resealable bag and refrigerate until chilled, about 1 hour.

(Continued on next page)

2. Snip off a small corner of the bag and fill the rigatoni. Arrange the rigatoni in a single layer as tightly as possible in a baking pan sprayed with non-stick spray. Pour mushroom cream sauce over the rigatoni until almost totally covered. Cover with foil and bake at 325°F (160°C) about 45 minutes.

MUSHROOM CREAM SAUCE

> 3 ounces (85 g) unsalted butter
> 8 ounces (227 g) cremini mushrooms
> 2 ounces (57 g) frozen porcini mushrooms
> 1 onion, thinly sliced
> 3 cloves of garlic, smashed
> ½ cup (119 mL) Marsala wine
> 1 cup (237 mL) turkey stock
> 1 cup (237 mL) heavy cream
> 1 sprig thyme
> Salt, to taste

1. Melt the butter in a large skillet. Add the mushrooms and sauté until caramelized. Add the onion and garlic and sauté until the onion is very soft, adding a splash of water, if needed.

2. Deglaze the skillet with the wine and reduce until syrupy. Add the stock and cook until reduced by half. Stir in cream and cook until the liquid is reduced by half. Add the thyme and let stand 20 minutes. Season to taste with salt and strain through a fine-mesh sieve. (The sauce should not be too thick because it will thicken as it bakes in the oven.)

CREAM OF BOURBON RED TURKEY NOODLE SOUP

By **Paul Virant**, Vie and Perennial Virant

4–6 SERVINGS

> 1 (10-pound [4.54-kg]) Bourbon Red Turkey
> 2 tablespoons canola oil
> 2 large onions, diced
> 3 stalks celery, diced

2 medium carrots, peeled and diced

1 head of garlic, split

1 tablespoon Herbes de Provence

Water

4 ounces (114 g) butter

3 Yukon Gold potatoes, peeled and quartered

Zest of 1 lemon

1 cup (237 mL) heavy cream

Salt and pepper

4 ounces (114 g) dried wide egg noodles, broken

½ cup (15 g) chopped Italian parsley

1. Breakdown the turkey into 2 breast halves, 2 legs and thighs, 2 wings, 1 neck, the carcass, and the giblets. (Reserve the breast for another use.)

2. Roast the parts, including giblets, drizzled with the oil in a baking pan at 400°F (200°C). When the turkey starts to brown, add 1 of the onions, 1 stalk celery, 1 of the carrots, the Herbes de Provence, and garlic. Roast until the turkey is brown and the vegetables are caramelized, about 1 hour.

3. Transfer everything to a stockpot and cover with water (3 to 4 quarts [2.37 to 3.80 L]), heat to boiling, and simmer 3 hours, removing the legs, thighs, and wings. Let cool, then remove the meat from the bones and reserve for garnish. When the stock is done, strain it and reserve.

4. Preheat a heavy soup pot over low heat, melt the butter, then add the remaining onion, 2 stalks of celery, 1 carrot, and season with salt and pepper. Cover and sweat until vegetables are tender. Add the potatoes and the reserved stock, heat to boiling, and simmer until the potatoes are tender. Add the cream and lemon zest and cook 5 minutes. Blend with an immersion blender until smooth. Season to taste and with salt and pepper and keep warm.

5. To serve, boil the noodles until tender, drain, and add to the soup along with the reserved meat and the parsley. Serve with crusty bread and salted butter.

CHAPTER 16

GENESIS GROWERS

Vicki Westerhoff | St. Anne, Illinois | genesis-growers.com

I t is July, and Vicki Westerhoff is walking the rows of her organic vegetable farm and thinking about onions. She started thinking about them in January, when she planted more than 300,000. But today many of them are being harvested, like the Tropea, a specialty onion from Italy popular with chefs because of its sweetness.

You can see the many varieties in various stages throughout the field. During the growing season, the stalks of the onions look healthy and vibrant. As the season goes on, they start to dry down, the stalks weaken and fall over, and the onion starts to form its skin for storage. That's when the work of harvesting those 300,000 onions begins.

"This is my 12th year and I started with just one acre," Vicki laughs; now she farms 55 acres with a team of nine workers, and is one of the most prolific small farms supplying restaurants and markets in Chicago. "It's very intensive, and I'm tired!" She laughs again but doesn't stop moving. She has incredible energy as she speeds around her fields, jumping from one thing to the next.

GROWING VEGETABLES FOR CHEFS

Vicki races through her crops, naming every plant by name. When you ask her how she remembers it all, she laughs yet again, "I don't know, I know everything."

"This celery, which I think is majorly gorgeous, I'm going to start harvesting for Nightwood," Vicki says. Celery is hard to grow because you have to "baby it" and make sure it stays well watered.

"I'm a specialty farmer, and a lot of what I do is custom growing. I try to grow the unusual thing and pick it when chefs want it at the size they want it," says Vicki, pointing to a row of carrots. "These carrots are by no means ready, but they're real small and some chefs want that size, so I pick them like that."

Colorful carrots are one of Genesis Growers signature items, and Vicki says they will do any size or shape the chefs want, and they sell them all winter long.

"Chefs like to cook with things that are fun and exciting, so if you don't have fun and exciting veggies, they have a hard time doing that," Vicki says, showing off Masego, a Japanese eggplant whose seed is difficult to get. "With my kind of farming, personal relationship is a big, big part of it."

When Vicki started going to Green City Market, she started to develop relationships with chefs. "They're kind of picky about who they work with, and it took a long time to gain trust with some of them," she says. Vicki now has the trust of restaurants like Nightwood, Lula Cafe, Carnivale, Uncommon Ground, David Burke's Primehouse, and many, many more.

GROWING ORGANICALLY

Vicki was working to grow those relationships while she was working to heal the land that was once planted in corn and soybeans. "When I started working on the farm, I discovered how damaged it was from being farmed industrially," says Vicki, who recently got her farm certified organic, but who has been growing organically since she started. "I had to heal the land, which had been depleted of nutrients."

Farming is a second career for Vicki, who once worked a desk job as an office manager, a job hard to imagine for someone as energetic as she is. In the late 1990s, to help heal health problems, including chronic fatigue syndrome, Vicki decided to start eating organically. When she couldn't find any organically grown produce in her local town, she decided to grow her own. She started out small, growing her own food on one acre of the 22 acres of land she lived on.

Both Vicki and her land have been revitalized, and she continues to be a steward of the land and of heirloom vegetable varieties that farmers like Vicki

Clockwise from top left: Just harvested tropea onions; Vicki is known for the 40 varieties of peppers that she grows; carrots ready for market; Vicki with her daughter, Angela, her son, Jon, and Jon's childhood friend and farmhand, Jay.

are helping to preserve. She saves many of her seeds, saying that a lot of the varieties she's grown in the past are no longer available from seed banks. It's important to save it each year to continue to grow those varieties. "We just have to keep working at preserving some of these things," she says, "so we can do our best to feed ourselves. I think that 'eat local' is going to become a necessity."

"Wow! That is really beautiful!" Vicki exclaims, passing by a row of brilliant purple and Thai basils, almost as if she's seeing it for the first time.

She comes to a handful of different types of cucumbers. "This is something that is really big among the chefs, all of our specialty cukes," she says. "Oh, and this chocolate pepper over here, these are so cool, they turn brown. And there are the mini bell peppers, too—chefs like to use those for stuffing."

Vicki grows about 40 different varieties of peppers, which are one of her specialties. Sweet peppers and also hot: Padron, shishito, mirasol, manzano, ancho, cayenne, and so many more.

Corn and beans, pumpkins and squash, beets and carrots, specialty lettuces, tomatoes—it is hard to find something that Vicki isn't growing in the field or in one of her five greenhouses. The greenhouses mean she can grow 12 months out of the year, even when snow covers her fields.

She is also trying to buy another 40 to 60 acres to put in perennial trees. She has been playing around with growing a few different fruit trees organically, but she hasn't had much luck so far. "When they say it's impossible to do organic fruit in the Midwest, it is," she says with a laugh.

In addition to supplying chefs and customers at Green City Market twice a week, Vicki is in charge of distributing her produce, as well as eggs and fruit from other local farms, to nearly 500 families in Chicago and northern Illinois who are part of her Community Supported Agriculture (CSA) program. Once you grasp the scale of how much Genesis Growers is producing, it's no wonder that Vicki never stops moving.

Two of her kids, Angela and John, as well as John's childhood friend, Jay, work on the farm full time and are often at Green City Market to help on market days. Vicki's crew of hired employees are nine set of hands to help with the massive amount of work—weeding and harvesting by hand—that is part of an organic vegetable farm.

"I am not a solo farmer, I am a team player, and these guys—well you can see," Vicki says, watching her workers gather together bunches of carrots for the weekend market. "Jose, he truly loves those carrots and kale and peppers and all of it. We talk a lot about sustainability, and sustainability goes a lot further than the issues we touch on. The sustainability of the lifestyle of the farmers and their employees is also huge."

FROM THE FARMER: Vicki Westerhoff

RECIPE

ROASTED WINTER SQUASH

This is one of my favorite recipes. Any squash can be used, but I like butternut, kabocha, or buttercup. Peel and chop potatoes into 1-inch (2.5-cm) chunks. Peel and chop the winter squash into 1-inch (2.5-cm) pieces. Chop 2 onions. Chop 2 red bell peppers and 2 green bell peppers. Finely dice 1 hot pepper. (I like to use a cayenne pepper.) Mix all the vegetables together in a roasting dish with a little olive oil or water. Cover and bake at 350°F (180°C) until tender, about 1 hour.

WISCONSIN TROUT SOUP WITH SOUR CREAM AND BACON

By **Jason Hammel**, Nightwood and Lula Cafe

4 SERVINGS

1 large trout (12 to 14 ounces [341 to 397 g])

2–3 slices streaky bacon (the fattier the better), minced

1 small onion, chopped

1 stalk celery, chopped

½ bulb of fennel, chopped

Salt and pepper

1 head of garlic, peeled, cloves sliced

½ teaspoon tomato paste

1 cup (237 mL) dry white wine

1 small splash orange juice or apple cider

1 quart (948 mL) fish, chicken, or vegetable stock
1 cup (237 mL) sour cream or crème fraîche
Fresh herbs, such as parsley, chervil, and marjoram
Potato Cream, for garnish
Chives, for garnish
Shredded cheddar cheese, for garnish

1. Fillet trout, reserving the head and discarding the skin and carcass.

2. Place the bacon in a heavy soup pot and cook over low heat to render the fat, but not crisp the bacon. Remove the bacon with a slotted spoon and reserve for garnish.

3. Add the onion, celery, and fennel, season with salt and pepper, and cook in the bacon fat over medium-low heat, stirring frequently, until the vegetables are soft but not brown. Add the garlic and cook until soft.

4. Add the tomato paste and cook 2 minutes, then add wine, and cook until mixture is dry, stirring frequently. Add the juice and cook until the mixture is dry, stirring frequently.

5. Add the stock, trout fillets and head, and heat to simmering over medium heat, skimming off the foam as it appears. Season lightly with salt and simmer until the liquid is reduced and has a pleasant fish flavor. Whisk in the sour cream, cook a few minutes, and season to taste with salt. Remove and discard the fish head. Meanwhile, prepare the Potato Cream and keep warm.

6. Puree the soup, in batches, in a food processor, adding a few fresh herb leaves with each batch. Strain the soup through a fine-mesh strainer.

7. To serve, divide the soup among 4 hot bowls, drizzle with the warm potato cream, garnish with the reserved bacon, the chives, and cheese.

POTATO CREAM

1 cup (237 mL) cream
3 small starchy potatoes, peeled

1. Bundle the potatoes in cheesecloth and tie bundle with kitchen string.

2. Place cream in small saucepan and heat over low heat. Submerge the bundle of potatoes in the cream and reduce the cream to about $^2/_3$ cup (158 mL).

3. Using the back of a large spoon, smash the potatoes a little to flavor the cream. Remove the bundle and add salt to the cream, to taste.

LIPSTICK PEPPERS STUFFED WITH GOAT CHEESE

By **Sarah Stegner and George Bumbaris**, Prairie Grass Cafe

4–6 SERVINGS

"Vicki, in my mind, is kind of a rock star when it comes to her peppers. She picks them at the perfect time and they are so intense in flavor—it's incredible. These peppers are bright red with thick flesh."—Sarah Stegner

6 small peppers, such as Lipstick
Salt and pepper
2 tablespoons olive oil
1½ cups (195 g) fresh goat cheese, room temperature
½ cup (75 g) chunky breadcrumbs, toasted
6 small handfuls of greens, such as arugula, basil, and mint
2 tablespoons aged or reduced balsamic vinegar (sweet)

1. Char the peppers over an open flame or on a gas grill, place in a bowl, and cover with plastic wrap. Let steam to help loosen the skin, 10 to 15 minutes. Rub peppers with a towel to remove the skins. Cut off the tops of the peppers and carefully remove the seeds.

2. Gently cook the peppers in olive oil in a medium skillet for a few minutes on each side. Season with salt and pepper. Remove the peppers from the skillet and cool.

3. Fill a piping bag with the goat cheese and pipe about 2 tablespoons of the cheese into each pepper. Place the peppers on a rimmed baking sheet and bake at 350°F (180°C), 10 to 15 minutes, or until the cheese is warm.

4. Arrange a handful of greens on each plate. Place the warm pepper in the center. Drizzle with balsamic vinegar and sprinkle with the toasted breadcrumbs.

CHAPTER **17**

SHOOTING STAR FARM

Rink DaVee and Jenny Bonde | Mineral Point, Wisconsin | greenandgreenfarms.com

Jenny is in the field harvesting green Bibb lettuce for Shooting Star's restaurant deliveries the next day. As she comes to a patch of lettuce that has been battered by a recent storm, she decides to skip over it.

Jenny Bonde and Rink DaVee grow vegetables on about five acres in Mineral Point, Wisconsin, where they specialize in lettuces. "Lettuce is one of our main crops," Rink says. "It's kind of what we are known for."

A big part of the quality of their lettuces is the way they handle them, from harvesting them meticulously, at the right time of day, to washing, cooling, and refrigerating them so that they store well.

Shooting Star stands out for the varieties they grow, too, like Little Gem, green Bibb, red Bibb, red oak, and radicchio. As Andrew Zimmerman, chef of Sepia in Chicago who uses a lot of what Jenny and Rink grow, puts it: "You can't really talk about Shooting Star and not talk about Rink's greens—the spicy mix is a constant favorite, and the arugula is great, as is Little Gem."

THE BEGINNINGS

Growing up in the suburbs of Chicago, Rink says he could think of nothing else but getting out of the city. In 1988 he got a job at Chez Panisse, working for Alice Waters, driving to pick up produce from farms. "That really opened my eyes to farming, and set me on this path," says Rink.

That path led him back to the Midwest in 1991, where he started working on Tapawingo Farm in Wisconsin, an organic farm ahead of its time that was sourcing to Chicago chefs, including Charlie Trotter and Rick Bayless.

Rink and Jenny met shortly after and started their own organic farm together on the land they bought in 1996. If there is an example of slow, steady
growth, it is Shooting Star Farm.

When Rink and Jenny bought their land, it was all pasture, without a tree or
a building in sight. During their first year farming the land, they built a greenhouse, a garden shed, and a tiny house—16 x 20 feet—where they lived for
seven years with no running water. "We didn't want to start building and get
into debt," Jenny says. "We started bare, bare bones, and scratched out a living."

"That first year that we were farming, even before we built that little house,
we were still living in town," Jenny says. "We would drive out to the farm, and
check on the vegetables and the greenhouse. We had built the garden shed,
and we would take turns sleeping in the shed at night; we had a wood-fired
greenhouse, so we had to stoke the fire in the middle of the night to make sure
it didn't get too cold."

In the winter, to save on the expense of plowing the road, they parked at the top of the hill and sledded down. Because they didn't have running water in their little house, they would stretch a hose from the packing barn where they prepped their produce to the little house.

"We were able to build really slowly because we lived an extraordinarily simple life for several years," Jenny says. "I'm grateful for that; some of it was really hard, but it makes for good story telling." Fifteen years later, they have a beautiful house—with running water—that they built with the help of friends, and where they live with their five-year-old son, Charlie.

WORKING WITH CHEFS

Early on, Jenny and Rink grew a following of chefs, from Bruce Sherman at North Pond, who makes a regular trip to the farm with his kitchen crew, to

Opposite page: Just-harvested beets are ready to be washed and prepped for delivery to Chicago restaurants. This page: Red Bibb lettuce ready to be picked; Rink DaVee and Jenny Bonde at Shooting Star Farm.

Jason Hammel of Lula Cafe and Nightwood. For many years Rink managed Home Grown Wisconsin, a farming cooperative that built relationships between chefs and farmers, and through which they met many more chefs. The co-op is now defunct, but Rink continues to coordinate getting produce from local farms to chefs in Chicago through his new business, Green & Green.

Rink and Jenny also sell locally at the Mineral Point Market. "That is really key for us to keep that balance," Rink says. "I have relationships with chefs, but it's also a farm that is bounded to the community here. It's all connected. The chefs help support us in growing unusual things, so we get to grow more of them; then we bring something like Lacinato kale to the market, where people will ask what it is and want to try it because they trust us."

"I had an event at the Ritz-Carlton, and that's the best feeling for me to know that my beets are put into some delicate terrine that the chef is making," Rink continues, "but that they were also sold that morning in Mineral Point for someone who wants to do pickled beets."

EVOLVING RELATIONSHIPS

When Rink first started farming in 1991, he was bringing heirloom tomatoes, salad mix, and unusual varieties of vegetables to chefs like Charlie Trotter and Rick Bayless. "They would say, 'We've never seen this before!' and they were flipping out over everything from candy-striped beets to the lettuces," Rink says. "Now 20 years later it's pretty hard to introduce a chef to something he doesn't know."

Rink says he sees an evolution, from the "I love it! How many can you get me!" reaction from chefs, to a period where chefs were asking farmers to grow specific vegetables for them. It didn't take long to realize that wasn't the best way, asking farmers to grow things that might not work well on their farms. The trust was put back on the farmer to grow what grows well and tastes good.

"We're not going to surprise these guys with stuff anymore," Rink says. "I see the next evolution as chefs coming up with a regional cuisine—and some already have started."

Clockwise from top left: Rink shows off a head of Bibb lettuce; Jenny picks heads to be delivered to chefs, which get loaded into their truck to be driven to their washing shed.

Jenny and Rink say they'd like the relationship between farmer and chef to grow further, where crop planning was done together to plan for the coming season. By taking into consideration what grows well on their farm, as well as what the chefs need in the year ahead, their hopes are that they could return to growing specialty items as they once did, having the support in advance from chefs.

"Five or six years ago we were just growing stuff and the Chicago movement was so voracious, chefs were sucking up quantities, so we weren't thinking about crop planning," Rink says. Jenny nods, "We were just doing it because they were taking it."

But some of what they were growing became speculative. "We would grow these wonderful things, but only sell half of it. Those were the things we love doing and we're going to bring them back," Rink says, "but we're going to have to reevaluate. We can't grow this specialty item and cross our fingers that on any given week someone is going to buy it from us. The seed is too expensive, the care that goes into it is too much."

By sitting down with chefs in advance of the growing season, before they have even put seeds in the ground, Rink and Jenny can get a sense of what the chefs will plan to use, and what they'd like to see them grow. They've already started discussions with Rick Bayless and Bruce Sherman, some of their longest standing relationships.

"Jenny passed over one crop of green Bibb today and started picking the next, and there is a big decision there," Rink says, "She passed over $400 of lettuce, but we're not in it to just sell it—we want to give these guys the best because they are going to pass that along to their customers."

"We feel a lot of camaraderie with chefs," Jenny adds. "The long hours and creating a product—our professions are very similar in that way. You gotta love it; you can't do it if you don't."

GET A TASTE OF SHOOTING STAR FARM

BIG JONES

bigjoneschicago.com

THE ELYSIAN HOTEL

elysianhotels.com

FRONTERA GRILL

fronterakitchens.com

HOPLEAF

hopleaf.com

NORTH POND

northpondrestaurant.com

OSTERIA VIA STATO

osteriaviastato.com

THE RITZ-CARLTON CHICAGO

fourseasons.com

SABLE

sablechicago.com

SEPIA

sepiachicago.com

MINERAL POINT MARKET

mineralpointmarket.com

FROM THE FARMERS: **Rink DaVee | Jenny Bonde**

RECIPE

ROASTED BEET SALAD WITH MUSTARD VINAIGRETTE
4 SERVINGS

> 6–8 small beets of any color, scrubbed, tops trimmed to
>   1 inch (2.5 cm)
> **Olive oil**
> **Salt and pepper**
> ¼ cup (25 g) pecans
> 4 tablespoons (59 mL) white wine vinegar
> 1 tablespoon Dijon mustard
> ½ cup (119 mL) extra-virgin olive oil
> **Salt and pepper**
> 4 cups (120 g) baby salad greens
> ½ small Italian bottle onion, or sweet onion, thinly sliced
> ¼ cup (29 g) crumbled blue cheese

1. Place the beets on a sheet of heavy-duty foil, drizzle with a bit of olive oil, and season with salt and pepper. Fold the foil over the beets, place in a small baking dish, and roast at 375°F (190°C) until tender when pierced with a knife, about 45 minutes. Cool.

2. Meanwhile, toast the pecans in a small skillet over medium-low heat, tossing frequently to prevent burning. Cool, then finely chop them.

3. When beets are cool enough to handle, use a paper towel (or fingers if you don't mind staining) to remove the peels, stems, and roots of beets. Cut beets into quarters. (Beets can stain your hands.)

4. To prepare the vinaigrette, combine the vinegar and mustard in a bowl. Whisk in the oil until emulsified. Season to taste with salt and pepper.

5. Toss the salad greens in a medium bowl with a small amount of the vinaigrette. Toss beets with a small amount of the vinaigrette in a separate bowl. Divide the greens between serving plates. Top with beets, onion, blue cheese, and pecans, and drizzle with as much more vinaigrette.

RADISH BUTTER

By **Bruce Sherman**, North Pond

> ½ pound (227 g) unsalted butter, softened
> Juice of ½ lemon
> Salt and pepper, to taste
> ¼ cup (6 g) chopped mint leaves
> 2 tablespoons snipped chives
> 2 tablespoons chopped Italian parsley
> 5 large Shooting Star Farm radishes, julienned

1. Beat the butter on medium speed of an electric stand mixer fitted with the paddle attachment. Beat in the lemon juice and season with salt and pepper. Beat in the chopped herbs until well blended. Carefully fold in the radishes. Season to taste with salt and pepper, and serve.

MUSTARD VINAIGRETTE WITH CHERVIL

By **Bruce Sherman**, North Pond

> 2 tablespoons sherry vinegar
> 2 tablespoons water
> 1 tablespoon Dijon mustard
> 1 teaspoon wildflower honey
> Salt and white pepper
> 1 teaspoon walnut or hazelnut oil
> ¼ cup (59 mL) olive oil
> ¼ cup (59 mL) sunflower or canola oil
> ¼ cup (8 g) chervil leaves (optional)

1. Whisk together in a small bowl, the vinegar, water, mustard, honey, and a pinch each of salt and pepper. Whisk in the walnut oil, then the olive and vegetable oils until emulsified. Season to taste with salt and pepper. Chop the chervil leaves and stir into the vinaigrette. Use the vinaigrette to dress mesclun salad greens.

ANISE HYSSOP SHERBET WITH CANDIED BEETS & ORANGE PEEL

By **Paul Fehribach**, Big Jones

4–6 SERVINGS

"The absolute and total care that Rink gives his plants is really second to none. You can get produce at any farmers' market that is delicious, beautiful and fresh, but what sets Rink apart is that his vegetables are almost coddled—they are really, really special. He knows just when to plant them, just how to seed them, when to space them, and when to weed them to grow plants that are stunningly beautiful."—Paul Fehribach

> **½ cup (119 mL) heavy cream**
> **2 cups (474 mL) plus ½ cup (119 mL) whole milk, divided**
> **⅔ cup (134 g) sugar**
> **½ teaspoon salt**
> **4 ounces (114 g) anise hyssop leaves**
> **Grated orange zest, for garnish**

1. Place the cream, ½ cup (119 mL) milk, and sugar in a heavy saucepan and gradually heat to simmering until the temperature reaches 165°F (74°C) on a thermometer. Remove from the heat and cool to room temperature for about 1 hour. Refrigerate overnight.

2. The next day, place the anise hyssop leaves in a blender and puree, using a small amount of the sugar and cream mixture to help liquefy the herb. When the anise hyssop is well pureed, with the blender running, pour in the remaining cream mixture in a thin steady stream, until the anise hyssop is completely liquefied and frothy, 5 to 8 minutes. Pour the mixture through a fine sieve, stir in the remaining 2 cups (474 mL) milk and the salt. Freeze in an ice cream maker according to the manufacturer's instructions. For best results, place the sherbet in the freezer for 2 to 4 hours to set before serving.

3. While the sherbet is in the freezer, prepare the Candied Beets. Serve the sherbet with the candied beets and grated orange zest.

CANDIED BEETS

8 ounces (227 g) beets, such as young Chioggia beets, peeled, cut into ¼-inch cubes

1 cup (227 mL) water

8 ounces (227 g) sugar

Pinch each: salt, pepper

1. Place all ingredients in a heavy-bottomed saucepan and gradually heat to simmering. (Do not boil.) Simmer gently 2 hours, or until beets are firm but cooked through. Cool about 1 hour before refrigerating. Store in its own syrup.

RED RUSSIAN KALE SALAD WITH MARCONA ALMONDS AND RADISHES

By **Andrew Zimmerman**, Sepia

4 SERVINGS

¼ cup (59 mL) olive oil

3 tablespoons (45 mL) unseasoned rice vinegar

2 tablespoons tamari (or soy sauce)

1 tablespoon plus 1 teaspoon mirin

1 tablespoon grated gingerroot

2½ teaspoons maple syrup

1½ teaspoons sesame oil

About 12 cups (780 g) loosely packed Red Russian kale, stems removed if tough, rinsed, thoroughly dried

6–8 radishes, thinly sliced

¼ cup (27 g) roughly chopped Marcona almonds

Salt and pepper, to taste

1. To prepare the sesame-ginger dressing, whisk together the olive oil, rice vinegar, tamari, mirin, gingerroot, maple syrup, and sesame oil in a small bowl.

2. Slice the kale thinly and place in a large bowl. Dress the kale with the dressing and massage it into the greens. Let the kale marinate for 30 minutes to 1 hour, depending on how mature or sturdy it is. Add the radish slices and almonds and toss to coat. Season to taste with salt and pepper.

PART 4

MOVING THE FARM TO THE CITY

The locally grown movement is here and has been for awhile, as shown by the chefs and farmers in this book. But progress continues, including efforts to bring the experience closer to the urban environment. From community-centric organizations like City Farm and Growing Power, to government-led examples like City Hall's rooftop garden and aeroponic food production within O'Hare International Airport, examples of urban growing are sprouting up all across the city. The three urban farms profiled here were created as parts of working restaurants, growing vegetables in collaboration with chefs' needs and desires. The growing trend of urban farming has taken roots in many restaurants in Chicago, including Browntrout, Carnivale, and North Pond, as well as the three profiled here, which have dedicated plots of earth or roof to grow, further shortening the distance food travels from farmer to chef.

CHAPTER **18**

THE BAYLESS GARDEN

Bill Shores | Chicago, Illinois | shoresgardenconsulting.com

One of the most consistent themes throughout Chicago's local food movement is the name of one chef: Rick Bayless. He sourced locally before there was even a movement, and he has been responsible for helping with the success of many of the small-scale growers in the Midwest, buying locally for his Frontera Grill, Topolobampo, and XOCO restaurants in River North, and giving grants to farmers through the Frontera Farmer Foundation. It's no surprise that a chef who champions local to the extent that he does has a production garden in his backyard.

The Bayless Garden was established 15 years ago, when Bayless wanted a vegetable garden to grow food for his restaurants. The lush green garden, grown on a full city lot, is also frequently used for entertaining. There is an outdoor kitchen where the chef's TV show, One Plate at a Time, is often filmed. Bill Shores, the urban gardener who manages the Bayless Garden, was hired to create a space with three purposes: a place that serves as a family's outdoor oasis; a site that can be used for a celebrity chef's TV show; and finally, a garden that produces food for the restaurants.

"It's a very multi-purpose garden," says Bill, who has been managing the garden for five years. "Rick wanted somebody who could take this 1,000-square-foot garden and make it produce in a more consistent way. My background growing for restaurants was pretty important to understand how to have consistent, high-quality yields."

At the Bayless Garden, things are planted densely, something Bill calls bio-intensive agriculture: a growing system that uses a minimal amount of space to get a large production.

Bill's first job farming was managing one-eighth of an acre producing several tons of food at Ohio University for a program in bio-intensive agriculture. His interest lay in urban agriculture and organic small-space gardening. He ended up going to graduate school in plant biology, but always focused on intensive agriculture.

"My mom was into house plants, my dad was an engineer, so there was that sort of scientific sort of background that was definitely an influence," Bill says. "A scientific, analytical way of looking at things fits in well with this kind of gardening; there is a lot of problem solving. Dealing with limited space, limited light, sometimes spaces are above ground level, like on decks or rooftops."

After ho got his degree in 1000, Dill started a market garden business called Green Edge Gardens, growing on a quarter acre and selling to restaurants and at farmers' markets in southeast Ohio. It grew to one acre as the demand from chefs grew. The local food movement around Ohio University was strong, with year-round farmers' markets and restaurants interested in using locally grown foods. He ran his business for seven years, and along the way got into growing microgreens in containers.

"I wanted a system for growing food year round, so I started in a heated greenhouse near my garden, and I grew salad greens in there year round," Bill says. "That was when micro greens were sort of a new thing; there weren't that many people doing them. I was focused on salad greens, which was my specialty. Restaurants can never get enough of salad greens, and they like the unusual stuff. And they liked the quality, freshness, and customization that I could provide for them."

When Bill moved to Chicago more than eight years ago, to be closer to his wife's family, he spent a couple of years working with a landscaper, followed by a year managing Growing Power's Grant Park garden. Soon after, he established his own business, working with clients to start urban gardens and doing "garden coaching" where he works alongside homeowners in their gardens. Through word of mouth, he was introduced to Bayless, who was looking for a new grower.

Bill starts his microgreens under this greenhouse-like structure of his design.

THE GARDEN

When Bill took over managing the garden, he made several changes to the layout in order to maximize growing space and take advantage of areas that weren't producing. The main part of the vegetable garden has full sun for the peak of the growing season, making it well-suited for food production. The Bloomingdale Line, a train line out of use and covered in Boston ivy, creates a wall along the north side of the garden. "People said nothing would grow up here, next to this, but that didn't make sense to me," Bill says. The area next to the wall is one of the sunniest. "I put in a pathway, made a raised bed in order to separate the roots of the ivy vines and the roots of the crops, to take advantage of this warm sunny microclimate." It's now home to robust, densely grown butternut squash that provides consistent squash blossoms, an essential ingredient in the restaurants.

Opposite page: heirloom tomatoes ready for Frontera; Bill plants dense beds of greens at the Bayless Garden. This page: young hanging butternut squash; *hoja santa's* fragrant leaves are a staple at the restaurant.

Along with changing the layout of the garden, Bill also set up a centralized worm-composting system for food waste. In multiple bins, worms turn over food scraps and create compost for the garden, at least 700 pounds of it. On the other side of the garden, Bill composts yard waste, which is free of food waste. Compost is an important element to container gardening, because the soil needs a constant renewal of nutrients.

Bill grows lots of herbs in pots and beds throughout the garden, including hoja santa. An important crop for the restaurant, it is a Mexican herb whose large leaves are fragrant and are used as a wrap around fish or tamales. The stems can also be chopped up to use in cooking. Bill grows hoja santa in four

different parts of the garden. He says it was difficult to track down, and now that he has it, he propagates more plants from the cuttings.

Bill's specialty, salad greens, is an essential crop in the Bayless Garden. He plants his greens very closely, three inches (7.5 cm) apart, which creates an appealing visual pattern. Solid blocks of crops look like a patchwork quilt. Bill broadcasts the seeds across the bed, they fall into prepared rows and are lightly covered with soil. When they start growing, you can't see the soil beneath them anymore, an effect that keeps the soil cool and moist and minimizes the weeds, which don't get sunlight beneath the canopy of lettuce.

In addition to planting densely, Bill grows using succession planting. The beds are constantly planted, harvested, and replanted very quickly, often every three weeks.

Bill is also in charge of 80 EarthBox containers, a self-watering container system, on the rooftop of Rick's three restaurants, where tomatoes and peppers grow for a rooftop salsa project. Four types of chili peppers, eight types of tomatoes and two herbs are being grown for the salsa.

But Bill's focus for the garden behind the house is salad greens, herbs, and edible flowers. He is growing thyme, lavender, oregano, epazote, seven different kinds of mint, flat-leaf parsley, nasturtiums, and edible marigolds. Year round, Bill grows a variety of microgreens, including mizuna, mustard greens, cilantro, and amaranth.

His harvest includes a few heirloom tomato varieties, squash and squash flowers, a few chili peppers, long beans, New Zealand spinach and chard.

A greenhouse on the second floor of the Bayless house is used in the winter to store plants, which are hoisted up and down with a winch Bill had put in when he started working in the garden.

The setup Bill has is an urban farmer's dream: "Rick subsidizes all of the materials, the seeds, the soil, but then buys what we grow." It is extra incentive for Bill to grow good, delicious crops, and gives him some autonomy to grow and sell to a chef just as he might if he were growing on his own land, rather than in Rick Bayless's backyard. This is a key component in the success of the garden and is evidence that urban farming can be viable, not just a pet project or side-show operation.

FROM THE FARMER: Bill Shores

RESOURCES AND INSPIRATION

The Vegetable Garden by Vilmorin-Andrieux. This is a good reference from the 1800s, with information on cultivating a wide variety of both common and uncommon food crops.

Growing Media for Ornamental Plants and Turf by Kevin Handreck and Neil Black. It's the go-to reference manual for container growing, indoor gardening, raised beds, above-ground gardening, et cetera.

Residential Landscape Architecture by Norman K. Booth and James E. Hiss. Good basic manual on landscape design.

Fine Gardening magazine has informative articles and photographs pertaining to both edibles and ornamentals.

Frontera Farmer Foundation was established by Rick and Deann Bayless to support local food production. One hundred percent of the proceeds go to provide capital grants to small Midwest farms.

RECIPE FOR POTTING MIX

FOR CONTAINER GARDENING, INDOOR SALAD AND MICROGREENS, AND RAISED BED GARDENS

All quantities measured by volume:
5 parts sifted peat moss or medium grade coir (coconut)
4 parts sifted mature compost
2 parts perlite (fine grade)
Organic granular fertilizer: ½ cup per each 5 gallons

ENSALADA DE HONGOS ASADOS CON ESPINACAS Y CHORIZO O TOCINO

(Roasted Mushroom Salad With Spinach and Chorizo or Bacon)

By **Rick Bayless**, Frontera Grill, Topolobampo, and XOCO

4 SERVINGS

To make this dish more substantial, crumble goat cheese over the finished salad, or serve it with a piece of good ripe cheese (and a crusty loaf of bread).

> 1 cup (8 ounces [227 g]) packed fresh Mexican chorizo sausage, casing removed OR 8 thick slices bacon, cut crosswise into ¼-inch (6-mm) pieces
>
> 4 cups (8 ounces [227 g]) sliced mushrooms, such as shiitakes, oysters, chanterelles, hedgehogs, alone or in combination
>
> 1 large red onion, cut into about ¼-inch-thick (6-mm) slices
>
> 8 cups (about 8 ounces [227 g]) spinach
>
> 3 tablespoons (45 mL) olive or vegetable oil
>
> 2 tablespoons fresh lime juice
>
> ½ teaspoon dried oregano, preferably Mexican
>
> Salt

1. Break the loose chorizo into small clumps (or scatter the bacon pieces) on a rimmed baking sheet. Sprinkle the mushrooms and onion over the top. Roast at 425°F (220°C) on the center oven rack. Stir after 10 minutes, breaking up any clumps of chorizo, then continue roasting until the onion is richly browned and the sausage (or bacon) is fully cooked, about 10 minutes more.

2. While the mushrooms are roasting, place the spinach into a large bowl.

3. To prepare the dressing, combine the olive oil, lime juice, oregano, ½ teaspoon salt, and 2 tablespoons water in a small microwaveable container. Microwave on high in for 30 seconds.

4. When the roasted mushroom mixture is ready, sprinkle it over the spinach. Drizzle the warm dressing over the salad and toss to coat. Serve immediately.

Variation: Roast, then peel, seed, and slice a couple of poblano chilies and add to salad. For a rich sweetness, replace the lime juice with balsamic vinegar; add 1 or 2 finely chopped canned chipotle chilis to the dressing for smoky spiciness.

TACOS DE ACELGAS GUISADAS CON CREMA

(Tacos of Creamy Braised Chard, Potatoes, and Poblanos)

By **Rick Bayless**, Frontera Grill, Topolobampo, and XOCO

MAKES ABOUT 4 CUPS (948 ML) OF FILLING, ENOUGH FOR 16 TO 18 SOFT TACOS

12 ounces (341 g) (4 medium-large) fresh poblano chili peppers

Scant 1 tablespoon vegetable or olive oil

1 medium white onion, sliced ¼-inch (6-mm) thick

2 garlic cloves, peeled and finely chopped

¼ teaspoon dried oregano, preferably Mexican

⅛ teaspoon dried thyme

16 to 18 corn tortillas (plus a few extra, in case some break)

¾ cup (178 mL) chicken broth

3 medium (about 10 ounces [284 g] total) red-skin boiling potatoes, cut into ½-inch (13-mm) cubes

6 cups loosely packed, sliced red or white chard leaves (slice them ½-inch [13-mm] thick; you'll need a 12-ounce [341-g] bunch)

½ to ¾ cup (119 to 178 mL) whipping cream or créme fraîche

½ teaspoon salt

½ to ¾ (114 to 170 g) crumbled Mexican queso fresco or pressed, salted farmer's cheese (optional)

1. To prepare 1½ cups (356 mL) of the Essential Roasted Poblano Rajas, roast the chili peppers directly over a gas flame or 4 inches (10 cm) below a very hot broiler until blackened on all sides, about 5 minutes for open flame, or about 10 minutes for broiler. Cover with a kitchen towel and let stand 5 minutes. Peel, pull out the stem and seed pod, then rinse briefly to remove bits of skin and seeds. Slice into ¼-inch (6-mm) strips.

2. Heat the oil over medium heat in a large (10- to 12-inch [25- to 30-cm]) skillet, then add the onion and cook, stirring frequently, until nicely browned but still a little crunchy, about 5 minutes. Add the garlic and herbs, toss a minute longer, then stir in the chili peppers.

3. To warm the tortillas, set up a steamer (with this many tortillas, you'll need 2 vegetable steamers set up in saucepans or a big Chinese steamer—either choice with ½ inch (13 mm) of water under the steamer basket); heat to boiling. Wrap the tortillas in 2 stacks in heavy kitchen towels, lay in the steamer(s) and cover tightly. Boil 1 minute, turn off the heat and let stand without opening the steamer(s) for about 15 minutes.

4. While the tortillas are steaming, prepare the filling. Combine the broth and potatoes in a small saucepan, cover, and simmer over medium-low heat until nearly tender, about 15 minutes.

5. Pour the potatoes and broth into the skillet with the rojas, mix in the chard, and boil over medium-high heat until the broth has evaporated, about 4 minutes. Stir in the cream and continue to boil, stirring frequently, until the cream is reduced enough to coat the mixture nicely. Season to taste with salt.

6. Scoop the mixture into a warm, deep serving dish, sprinkle with the cheese, if desired, and carry to the table along with the warm tortillas in a cloth-lined basket for each of your guests to assemble tacos *al gusto*.

Advance Preparation: The poblano rajas can be made several days ahead but it is best to finish the filling shortly before serving.

Variations: Serve over grilled chicken; replace the cream with ¼ to ⅓ cup (59 to 79 mL) yogurt (just heat it through, but don't boil or it will curdle); or don't reduce the cream, stir in a little chopped ham and toss with cooked egg noodles or bow-tie pasta and sprinkle with lots of chopped cilantro before serving.

CHAPTER 19

PLEASANT FARMS

Morgan Kalberloh | Chicago, Illinois | pleasantfarmschicago.com

Pleasant Farms is growing a community in the neighborhood. It also happens to supply Pleasant House Bakery with weekly produce, year-round, grown by urban farmer Morgan Kalberloh. Pleasant House Bakery is a casual, cozy corner restaurant with a menu of savory, simple English-style pies, run by Morgan's sister Chelsea, and her husband, chef Art Jackson.

Morgan's vegetables make an impact on the food served at the bakery, which benefits from fresh ingredients grown nearby. But his vegetables are also influencing the community of people who live in the neighborhood, who walk by and see him farming in an urban setting. Morgan says the people are as much a part of it for him as the farming is. Like the Spanish woman who passes by regularly and asks him what he is growing; or the guy from a rough part of the neighborhood who, passing by Morgan tending to his crop, stopped in his tracks and said, "This made my day."

Morgan was living in Florida, where he received his master's degree in biogeography, and was in the process of setting up an arboretum at Florida State University, when Chelsea and Art found a spot to start their business, a business the three of them had talked about for nearly 10 years. In the fall of 2010 they started building out a corner space in Bridgeport with the help of architect friends. They also started building an urban garden down the road. Art's brother built a trio of 4 x 12-feet wood frames, and Morgan started ordering seeds.

GROWING

Morgan grows cucumbers, tomatoes, eggplants, arugula, braising greens, beet greens, spinach, red butterhead lettuce, mustard greens, specialty Chinese greens, red Russian fingerling potatoes, tomatoes, and much more.

He says he is able to grow this variety in such a small space with succession farming, where there is always something ready to plant when a crop is coming out. The turnover rate is quick. Morgan grows organically, which means he brings in organic soil to fill above-ground containers, and enriches it with peat and organic compost.

During the winter, the wooden structures are covered with UV-transmitting plastic, which protects the plants but allows for continued growth. Morgan

overwinters the vegetables that can freeze and withstand the cold, like mustard greens, endive, hearty kale, bunching onions, and carrots. But his goal, and challenge, is to have produce available to the bakery year round.

"It's a learning curve," Morgan says. "That's the cool thing about farming: You never stop learning because no season is ever the same.

"In the city people talk about not being able to feed people, but that's just a bunch of crap," Morgan says. "Look at all of this land space, on top of every single building. It doesn't have to be every single building, but even if we used one of every five houses no one would go starving."

The challenge urban dwellers face may not be space, but the *how-to*. Morgan has recently starting giving classes on urban farming, teaching others what comes so naturally to him: how to grow food. He wants to encourage

people to learn how to grow front-yard gardens, and to start a conversation with others in the neighborhood.

"It's not like we've evolved away from growing things," he says. "No one really farms anymore, but people still get it."

Morgan teaches how to build raised beds, how to start seeds, how to transplant seedlings into the soil, all using his organic farming methods. "There used to not be a word for organic, because it just was the way it was," Morgan says. "We're two generations separated from not having a name for it, to today where it is the little guy."

Morgan is building a small farming community of people who are talking about farming and gardening in the city, the way he hopes the word, and activity, will spread.

FOOD FOR THE COMMUNITY

"I've always been an idealist, and I think there is no reason why we can't make a restaurant more of a community-focused operation," Art says, "where we can take kids to the garden to teach them and then bring them back to the restaurant. From day one, that community happened naturally."

Morgan is on the same page. "I told my sister I'm not coming here just to do some farming," he says. "It's got to involve people because, as a geographer, that's really the main thing in my world."

Morgan calls Bridgeport "the community of the future," an area of Chicago once home to slaughterhouses and the most polluted branch of the Chicago River, now home to urban farming sites. "There are all these urban farms going in," he says. "Growing Power, The Plant, us, and all of these community gardens and front-yard gardens."

Another one of Pleasant Farms' sites is on Iron Street, next to an enormous warehouse. The owner of the building—with hopeful ideas about how to make positive change in the neighborhood—heard about Pleasant House Bakery, liked what they were doing, and approached Art, Chelsea, and Morgan to see if they'd like to plant a garden behind his building.

Art says a garden that supplies the restaurant has always been an essential element to their business. "By keeping the restaurant small, we would be able to have a garden nearby—that was essential to whatever concept we pursued."

Art grew up an hour west of Chicago, where his mom grew food in a big garden, baked bread, canned vegetables, and greatly influenced Art in what he wanted to do. He started cooking from her *Gourmet* magazines, and pretty early on, decided he wanted to be a chef.

"My grandma said to me when I was 12, 'Well if you want to be a chef, you should open a pie shop like my friend in New Zealand.' I said, 'Oh grandma, I'm going to be a fancy French chef,'" Art remembers. "But when it came to our own concept, it seemed like keeping it simple really made a lot of sense." So he opened a pie shop.

He says his hope is to elevate simple food to a level where people are going to realize and appreciate the fresh ingredients, but still keep it accessible.

"Art is a very talented chef and could have easily run a fancy restaurant where he charged $30 a plate, but he is doing this pie, this simple homemade food that is for everyone," Morgan says. "There would be no hope for us if it wasn't. We just want to smile and say hello and have people come in and change things in a very simple sort of way."

FROM THE FARMER: Morgan Kalberloh

RESOURCES AND INSPIRATION

BOOKS

I'm always fascinated by **Mel Bartholomew's PBS show and his book**, *All New Square Foot Gardening*, is a great resource for beginners and urban gardeners using raised beds.

In Partnership with Nature **by Jochen Bockemühl**. Bockemühl is a student of Goethe and Ruldolf Steiner and he explores biodynamics and experiential science of the material and spiritual.

Ecology and economics cannot be separated. *The Ecological Revolution: Making Peace with the Planet* by John Bellamy Foster explores the dangers of commodifying nature.

Rodale's *Encyclopedia of Organic Gardening*, first published in 1959. The information will never get old, what is old is new!

The New Organic Grower: A Master's Manual of Tools and Techniques for the Home and Market Gardener by Eliot Coleman gives experiential knowledge of a diverse market gardener.

WEBSITES

Attra.org is an organization for sustainable agriculture; it has a great publications list for sustainable farming techniques.

JSTOR.org has scholarly, peer-reviewed literature.

Johnnyseeds.com sells seeds but also offers growing tips and the supported research and trials of many diverse seeds.

MonthlyReview.org, an independent Socialist magazine, offers articles on Marxist ecology.

Anthromedia.com/en/ is a website about Anthroposophy (a philosophy founded by Rudolf Steiner).

State and County Extension Services websites are a great resource for local gardening knowledge and agricultural research.

FILMS

The Gleaners and I is about gleaning, both historic and modern versions.

I Like Killing Flies is about a small restaurant owner in Brooklyn who just makes good stuff. A weird guy, neat story.

The Real Dirt about Farmer John is about the trials and tribulations of a small farmer in the United States.

MUSHROOM AND KALE PIE

By **Art Jackson**, Pleasant House Bakery

4–6 SERVINGS

8 ounces (227 g) Russian or black kale (or a combination)
2 ounces (57 g) plus 1 ounce (28 g) unsalted butter, divided
5 ounces (142 g) shallots, thinly sliced
8 ounces (227 g) cremini mushrooms, sliced
8 ounces (227 g) shiitake mushrooms, sliced
1 head roasted garlic
2 ounces (57 g) all-purpose flour
4 ounces (120 mL) white wine
1 quart (948 mL) plus 1 tablespoon milk, divided
3 ounces (85 g) grated Parmesan cheese
Salt and pepper, to taste
Pie crust dough for a double 9-inch (22.5-cm) crust*
1 egg

Store-bought puff pastry can be substituted. Instead of a pie with a double crust, use the puff pastry just on top.

1. Remove the stems from the kale and tear the leaves into 1-inch (2.5-cm) pieces. Cook the kale in a large pot of rapidly boiling salted water until tender, about 5 minutes. Remove with a strainer and set aside. Gently squeeze kale in strainer with the back of a spoon to remove most of the water.

2. Heat a large skillet over medium heat and add 1 ounce (28 g) of butter. Add shallots and sauté until they begin to soften, about 5 minutes. Add the mushrooms and sauté until they release all of their water. Continue to sauté until mushrooms are dry. Add the remaining 2 ounces (57 g) butter and roasted garlic, then stir in the kale. Stir in the flour. Stir in the wine and cook 5 minutes. Add the milk, stirring until well blended. Cook and stir the mixture another 5 minutes. Stir in the cheese and season to taste with salt and pepper. Remove from the heat and cool to room temperature. Stew can be refrigerated a day ahead at this point.

3. To assemble the pie, roll out half of the pie dough and line a 9-inch (22.5-cm) pie pan. Fill with the mushroom mixture. Roll the remaining dough and cover the filling, crimping the edge. Beat the egg in a small bowl and beat in the milk. Brush the egg mixture over the top crust. Bake at 350°F (180°C) for 45 minutes to 1 hour, or until the filling is hot and the crust is golden brown.

CHAPTER 20

UNCOMMON GROUND ROOFTOP FARM

Dave Snyder | Chicago, Illinois | uncommonground.com

When you're standing in the middle of Uncommon Ground's rooftop farm, sounds of screeching brakes and sirens substitute for crickets and birds. Tall buildings replace a backdrop of trees. But just like other organic farms throughout the Midwest, it's a working farm that grows produce for chefs; in this case, the chef right downstairs at Uncommon Ground restaurant.

Uncommon Ground was the country's first certified organic rooftop farm in 2008, when owners Michael and Helen Cameron opened their second restaurant in the Edgewater neighborhood of Chicago. The 2,500-square-foot expanse is taken up with planter boxes filled with what chef Chris Spear and farmer Dave Snyder have planned together.

GROWING IN THE CITY

Dave has been Uncommon Ground's rooftop farmer for two seasons. When he first moved to Chicago from Seattle eight years ago, there was a community garden across the street from his apartment called the Ginkgo Organic Garden.

"Usually with a community garden, you have your plot and I have mine, but everything at Ginkgo is gardened cooperatively," Dave says, "and then the entire harvest gets donated to this food bank for low income folks with AIDS. It's a really nice match because we're providing high quality organic produce for a population that has to look after its general health very carefully."

Dave learned how to plant, grow, and harvest from volunteering at the community garden. Since he started at Uncommon Ground, he has been growing lettuces, herbs, tomatoes, spinach, peas, kale, mustard greens, sorrel, radishes, ground cherries, and more. Urban farming challenges include space, of course, and the nutrients in the soil. Dave says he tries to limit the crops that take a long time to grow so that planters aren't taken up with vegetables for a big chunk of the season. Instead he likes to plant lettuces and greens he can harvest multiple times throughout the season, along with other high-turnover crops. Dave composts "religiously" so he can enrich the soil in the container boxes, a necessity because nutrients are depleted quickly.

CHICAGO RARITIES ORCHARD PROJECT

Dave got connected with the Camerons through the Chicago Rarities Orchard Project. When he heard that the farmer of Uncommon Ground was leaving, he got in touch with them to start farming the rooftop.

The Chicago Rarities Orchard Project is aimed at starting community orchards in the city, in particular rare and endangered varieties of fruit. Dave is one of a handful of people heading up the project. "One hundred years ago, there were 15,000 different kinds of apples just in America—forget about Asia where apples come from—and in the last 100 years we have lost 85 to 90 percent of those," Dave says. "When you lose a variety, you lose the flavor, the texture, the aroma, how you use it, it's resistance to disease and pests, the ability for it to grow in different climates; when you lose a variety, you lose its genetic abilities."

They plan to plant the first orchard in Logan Square in the summer of 2012, starting with between 20 to 40 varieties, including apple, cherry, plum, and peach trees, as well as paw paws, medlars, and persimmons.

Dave says there is a pressing need to preserve varieties that are still in existence. Whether planting fruit trees, growing on the rooftop, or cultivating and growing in many acres of farmland, diversity is important, and actually crucial to food safety, according to Dave.

STRENGTH IN DIVERSITY

"The idea is that diversity builds robustness," Dave says. "It doesn't matter if you are talking about financial investments or food systems: the more diversity you have, the stronger the system."

There are 200,000 different kinds of wheat, Dave says, pointing out that he can't even name two types. "Most industrialized agriculture is monoculture,

The rooftop garden sits above Uncommon Ground restaurant in the Chicago neighborhood of Edgewater.

or very close to monoculture, and the weakness of monocultures has been proven time and time again," he says. The most dramatic example is the Irish potato famine.

"It's something that mathematicians study as much as ecologists study. If you grow only one kind of your crop, then it had all the strengths of that variety, but it also has all of the weaknesses too," he says.

"They were only growing a single species of potatoes that was easy to propagate, but that meant that the genetic variation of all of those potatoes was essentially nothing and so when potato blight made it to Ireland, the crops were decimated," Dave explains. "Of course, potato blight came to the United States too, but it didn't decimate America's potato crop because we had far more potato varieties at that time."

SMALL SCALE DIVERSITY

On the rooftop, Dave grows as many varieties of vegetables he can, including unusual heirloom varieties that might not be found at many other farms. Because the crop planning is collaborative between chef and farmer, chef Chris Spear can hand-pick nearly anything that Dave says will grow well in their conditions. Before ordering seeds, well before planting anything, Dave sits down with Chris to plan for the growing season ahead.

"It's totally collaborative and it has to be, because it doesn't do me any good to grow something that he doesn't need," Dave says. "He thinks about things from an ingredient point of view.; I know what is efficient to grow."

When chefs work through a large distributor, there may be three types of tomatoes they sell, a slicing, a paste, and a cherry tomato. When chefs go to farmers' markets, the farmers are selling dozens of varieties of tomatoes. "If you're a small grower, you could grow a thousand different kinds of tomatoes," Dave says, "And in our situation, Chris has access to all of those different varieties, provided that we plan ahead."

Like the Purple Calabash.

"The Purple Calabash is actually a wonderful tomato, but you can see just by looking at it, it's super duper delicate, it breaks really easily and most farmers would never bother with it," Dave says.

Even though the tomato has wonderful flavor, it's a terrible crop to grow and transport, and for local farms growing enormous varieties of tomatoes, this specific one probably wouldn't be worth the trouble. Because Uncommon Ground's scale is so much smaller, and primarily because they don't have transportation in their system, they can grow something like the Purple Calabash and get it to the chef and onto the menu.

"We feed on average 100 people a day. If you imagine a sustenance farm of a half acre to an acre for one family, and you have a family of 100 people, you can imagine our farm would have to be pretty large," Dave says. "This is actually one one-hundredth of one acre. It's a very small proportion of the food the chef uses, but we can grow certain very special things that are difficult to source elsewhere, which is pretty neat."

Clockwise from top left: Dave lets lettuce go to seed, which he saves for next year's planting; succession planting helps allow fast-growing crops to be moved in and out of the containers on the roof; flowers and herbs grow alongside vegetables and lettuces; Dave Snyder among his plants.

FROM THE FARMER: **Dave Snyder**

RESOURCES AND INSPIRATION

In terms of urban agriculture, nothing has inspired me more than **Ginkgo Organic Gardens**, where I volunteer. It is a cooperatively farmed community garden that donates its harvest to a foodbank. It is Ginkgo that originally interested me in growing and Ginkgo that continues to remind me why we're doing what we're doing.

Other sources of inspiration are **City Farm** and **Kilbourn Park Organic Greenhouse**. It's the people and the projects that get me most excited.

GRILLED TROUT STUFFED WITH TOMATO CONFIT

By **Chris Spear,** Uncommon Ground

4 SERVINGS

> 2 pounds (908 g) cherry tomatoes
> 1 lemon
> 4 cups (948 mL) tomato juice
> 4 trout, headless (8 to 10 ounces [227 to 284 g] each)
> ⅓ cup (10 g) packed parsley leaves, chopped
> 2 sprigs tarragon, chopped
> 8 chives, minced
> Salt and pepper
> Vegetable oil

1. To prepare the tomato confit, slice the cherry tomatoes as thinly as possible, about ⅛ inch (3 mm). Place tomato slices in a baking dish big enough where you can layer the tomatoes in bottom of dish (double layer if necessary). Pour tomato juice over tomatoes and enough water until tomatoes are just submerged in liquid. Cover dish with foil and roast at 250°F (120°C) 2 hours or until tomatoes are very soft. When tomatoes are finished cooking, remove from the oven and cool in the liquid. Carefully transfer the tomatoes to a bowl using a slotted spoon.

2. To prepare the trout, squeeze 1 lemon into 1 gallon (3.80 L) of water. Dip the trout into the lemon-water to get rid of the slimy membrane on the skin. Dry well with paper towels. Place in refrigerator until ready to go on the grill.

3. Preheat the grill for direct cooking. Oil the grid.

4. Open each trout, meat side up. Sprinkle with herbs, evenly distribute the tomato confit onto the trout, and season with salt and pepper. Close the trout.

5. The grill is ready when you cannot put your hand 4 inches (10 cm) from the grid for 5 seconds. Oil the skin and carefully place the trout on the grid with the open flaps facing you. Grill until the trout skin releases from the grid, 5 to 6 minutes. Carefully turn the trout so the openings are facing up. This will ensure the tomato confit will not fall out of the trout. Grill 5 to 6 minutes on the second side. You can open the trout to make sure the trout is cooked thoroughly as the meat near the spine will take the longest.

SEARED ALASKAN SALMON
By **Chris Spear**, Uncommon Ground

4 SERVINGS

> **Basil Oil (recipe follows)**
> **Green Goddess Dressing (recipe follows)**
> ¼ cup (75 g) salt
> 1 cup (145 g) English peas, shelled
> 2 cups (126 g) sugar snap peas
> 4 (6-ounce [170-g]) Alaskan salmon fillets
> About 4 tablespoons (59 mL) oil
> Salt and pepper
> 2 tablespoons minced shallots
> 2 tablespoons blended oil (25% olive oil and 75% canola oil)
> 3 ounces (90 mL) vegetable stock
> 8 large basil leaves

1. Begin to prepare the Basil Oil the day before serving (it is a 2-day process). Prepare the Green Goddess Dressing the day before serving.

2. Fill a large pot with water and ¼ cup (75 g) salt and heat to boiling. Fill a large bowl with ice water. Drop the shelled peas into the boiling water for 45 seconds and immediately transfer to the ice water with a strainer. When peas are cool, take them out of ice water, and let dry on a cloth towel. Repeat the same process with the sugar snap peas.

3. Dry the salmon fillets with paper towels. Heat an ovenproof 12-inch (30-cm) skillet for 2 minutes on high heat. Add enough oil to coat the bottom of the skillet. Season the salmon on the flesh side with salt and pepper and gently place, skin side down, in the skillet. (Do not crowd.) Reduce heat to medium and cook until the salmon starts to brown around the edges. Without turning, place the skillet in a 350°F (180°C) oven and cook about 6 minutes. Salmon will be medium-rare to medium.

4. Remove salmon from the oven and carefully turn the fillets over. Let rest 30 seconds. Remove fillets to paper towels and let rest for 5 minutes. (Fillets will be crispy on one side and tender on the other.)

5. In a separate medium skillet, heat 2 tablespoons of the oil over medium heat and sauté the shallots for about 1 minute. Add the shelled peas, snap peas, and vegetable stock. Cook until the stock is evaporated. Roughly chop the basil and add to the skillet. Season to taste with salt and pepper.

6. To serve, place 2 to 3 tablespoons (30 to 45 mL) of the dressing on one side of each plate. With the back of a spoon smear it across each plate. Divide the vegetables among the plates over the dressing. Place salmon fillets on top of the vegetables. Drizzle basil oil around the vegetables and salmon. Serve immediately.

(Continued on next page)

BASIL OIL

2 ounces (57 g) basil
1 cup (237 mL) blended oil (25% olive oil and 75% canola oil)

1. On day 1, fill large saucepan half full of water and add a pinch of salt. Heat to boiling. While water is heating, remove basil leaves from stems, discarding stems. Drop basil into water, stir, and immediately remove the basil with a strainer. Run basil under cold water to cool. Carefully, squeeze excess water from basil. Place the basil into a blender, add oil, and process for 1 minute. Store in plastic container, covered, overnight.

2. On day 2, spread out cheesecloth, fold multiple times, and place over a drinking glass. Fasten the rubber band around the rim and let the cheesecloth sag about 2 inches (5 cm) into the glass. Slowly pour basil oil into cheesecloth. Return the basil oil to the refrigerator for a few hours. Strain the basil oil through the cheesecloth undisturbed. (Do not force the oil through cheesecloth or the sediment will get into the finished product, which will make the oil go bad more quickly.) When basil oil has all drained into the glass, discard the cheesecloth.

GREEN GODDESS DRESSING

½ cup (119 mL) mayonnaise
⅓ cup (79 mL) sour cream
½ half avocado
1 shallot, minced
1 garlic clove, minced
¼ cup (12 g) minced chives
¼ cup (8 g) minced parsley
¼ cup (8 g) minced tarragon
1 tablespoon lemon juice
1 teaspoon champagne vinegar
Salt and pepper, to taste

1. Place the mayonnaise, sour cream, and avocado into food processor and process until well blended. Transfer to a bowl. Add shallot, garlic, herbs, lemon juice, and vinegar, and mix well. Season to taste with salt and pepper. This dressing is always better the second day.

INDEX

RECIPE INDEX

ABOUT THE AUTHOR

Anna Blessing has created 14 editions of the *eat.shop/Rather* book series and been a regular contributor to many print and online publications, including Lucky magazine, where she was Chicago editor for six years. She lives in Chicago with her husband and daughter.